MASTERING THE ART

PROJECT MANAGEMENT

A Comprehensive Guide for Success

Wilfred Akins

TABLE OF CONTENT

INTRODUCTION

THE IMPORTANCE OF EFFECTIVE PROJECT MANAGEMENT

Effective project management is a critical component in today's dynamic and intricate business landscape. It serves as a guiding force for the successful completion of projects, regardless of their scale or complexity. Whether undertaking large-scale initiatives, implementing organizational changes, or handling individual tasks, project management plays a pivotal role. Its significance can be attributed to several key reasons.

Firstly, effective project management ensures the achievement of goals. By aligning projects with the broader objectives of an organization, project managers create a framework that promotes strategic consistency. They establish clear project objectives, define success criteria, and develop a comprehensive roadmap to guide the project's trajectory. This focused approach enhances the likelihood of project success and the delivery of desired outcomes.

Secondly, project management optimizes resource allocation. A well-executed project requires the efficient utilization of resources, including human capital, time, and budgetary allocations. Project managers meticulously plan and allocate resources based on project requirements, considering factors such as skill sets, availability, and dependencies. This thoughtful allocation helps prevent overutilization or underutilization of resources, ensuring their optimal use throughout the project lifecycle.

Another significant aspect of effective project management is risk mitigation. Projects inherently involve uncertainties and risks that can impede progress or result in failure. However, project management methodologies equip project managers with tools and techniques to identify, assess, and mitigate potential risks. By proactively managing risks, project managers minimize their impact on the project, increasing the likelihood of achieving project objectives within the defined constraints.

Furthermore, effective project management promotes collaboration and communication among project stakeholders. Project managers act as the focal point for information dissemination, facilitating effective communication channels between team members, stakeholders, and sponsors. This ensures that all relevant parties are kept informed about project progress, changes, and challenges. Open and transparent communication enhances team cohesion, mitigates conflicts, and fosters a shared understanding of project goals and expectations.

In addition to these benefits, effective project management helps manage project constraints, such as scope, time, and budget. Project managers carefully monitor and control these factors, ensuring that the project remains within its defined boundaries. They proactively identify and address deviations, making necessary adjustments to keep the project on track. This proactive approach minimizes the risk of scope creep, schedule delays, and budget overruns, thus safeguarding project success.

The importance of effective project management cannot be overstated. It serves as a linchpin for project success, ensuring the alignment of projects with organizational goals, optimizing resource allocation, mitigating risks, promoting collaboration and communication, and managing project constraints. By implementing robust project management practices, organizations can enhance their ability to execute projects efficiently, deliver desired outcomes, and achieve long-term success in an ever-evolving business landscape.

THE ROLE OF THE PROJECT MANAGER

The role of a project manager is pivotal in ensuring the successful execution and completion of projects. Project managers are responsible for overseeing all aspects of a project, from its initiation to its closure. Their role encompasses a wide range of responsibilities and skills, including:

Project Planning: Project managers are involved in the initial planning phase, where they define project objectives, scope, deliverables, and timelines. They create a comprehensive project plan that outlines the tasks, resources, and dependencies required for successful project execution. This plan serves as a roadmap for the project team and stakeholders.

Team Leadership: Project managers are responsible for leading and managing the project team. They assemble the right team members, assign roles and responsibilities, and provide guidance and support throughout the project. Effective project managers inspire and motivate their team

Communication and Stakeholder Management: Project managers play a crucial role in facilitating communication among project stakeholders. They act as a central point of contact, ensuring that information flows efficiently between team members, clients, sponsors, and other relevant parties. Project managers are skilled in stakeholder management, actively engaging and involving stakeholders throughout the project lifecycle to gather requirements, manage expectations, and address concerns.

Risk Management: Project managers are responsible for identifying and mitigating risks that may impact project success. They conduct risk assessments, identify potential threats and opportunities, and develop risk response strategies. Project managers continuously monitor risks throughout the project, implementing contingency plans and taking proactive measures to minimize their impact.

Budget and Resource Management: Project managers are accountable for effectively managing project budgets and resources. They monitor project expenditures, track costs, and ensure that the project stays within the allocated budget. Additionally, project managers oversee resource allocation, ensuring that the right resources are available at the right time and optimizing their utilization to achieve project goals.

Schedule and Progress Monitoring: Project managers closely monitor project schedules, ensuring that tasks are completed on time and milestones are achieved as planned. They track project progress, identify bottlenecks or delays, and take corrective actions to keep the project on track. Project managers also provide regular progress updates to stakeholders, keeping them informed about the project's status and any adjustments made.

Quality Assurance: Project managers are responsible for ensuring that project deliverables meet the required quality standards. They define quality criteria, establish quality control processes, and conduct regular quality reviews to ensure that project outcomes meet or exceed expectations. Project managers also address any deviations or issues related to quality promptly.

Change Management: In dynamic business environments, projects often encounter changes in requirements, scope, or circumstances. Project managers are adept at managing change, assessing its impact on the project, and implementing change management strategies. They communicate changes to the team and stakeholders, adjust project plans as needed, and ensure that the project remains adaptable and resilient.

Overall, the role of a project manager encompasses diverse responsibilities that require strong leadership, communication, problem-solving, and organizational skills. They serve as the driving force behind project success, ensuring effective planning, execution, and delivery while managing risks, resources, and stakeholder expectations. Through their expertise and guidance, project managers facilitate the achievement of project goals and the realization of desired outcomes.

CHAPTER 1

PROJECT INITIATION

Project initiation is the first phase in the project lifecycle, where the project is defined, authorized, and initial planning takes place. It sets the foundation for a successful project by clarifying the project's objectives, scope, and stakeholders' expectations. Here's an overview of the project initiation phase:

Project Identification:

Identify the need or opportunity for the project, whether it's driven by market demand, strategic objectives, or customer requirements.

Conduct a feasibility study to assess the project's viability, considering factors such as technical feasibility, financial viability, and organizational capacity.

Project Charter:

Develop a project charter, a formal document that outlines the project's purpose, objectives, deliverables, stakeholders, and high-level scope.

The project charter provides a clear mandate for the project and establishes the authority and responsibilities of the project manager.

Stakeholder Identification and Analysis:

Identify and engage stakeholders who are directly or indirectly affected by the project.

Conduct a stakeholder analysis to understand their interests, expectations, and influence on the project.

Develop a stakeholder management plan to define strategies for effective communication, engagement, and addressing stakeholder needs throughout the project.

Project Scope Definition:

Clearly define the project's scope, including the boundaries, objectives, deliverables, and exclusions.

Identify key project constraints and assumptions that may impact the project's scope and boundaries.

Project Team Formation:

Assemble a project team with the necessary skills, knowledge, and experience to execute the project.

Define roles, responsibilities, and reporting structures within the project team.

Initial Risk Assessment:

Identify and assess potential risks and uncertainties that may impact the project's success.

Develop an initial risk management plan to outline strategies for identifying, analyzing, mitigating, and monitoring project risks.

Project Planning:

Develop an initial project plan, outlining the high-level approach, major milestones, and key deliverables.

Identify and estimate the required resources, budget, and schedule for the project.

Identify dependencies and critical success factors to guide subsequent project planning and execution.

Project Governance:

Establish a project governance structure and define decision-making processes.

Determine how the project will align with organizational strategies, policies, and governance frameworks.

Project Approval:

Present the project charter, initial plan, and associated documents to key stakeholders or a project governance board for approval.

Obtain the necessary authorization and funding to proceed with the project.

Project Kickoff:

Conduct a project kickoff meeting to communicate project objectives, roles, responsibilities, and expectations to the project team and stakeholders.

Use the kickoff meeting to foster team collaboration, set expectations, and establish a shared understanding of the project's purpose and goals.

The project initiation phase is crucial for setting the right direction and establishing a solid foundation for the project. It lays the groundwork for effective planning, execution, and control throughout the project lifecycle. By investing time and effort in project initiation, organizations increase their chances of successful project outcomes and stakeholder satisfaction.

1.1 Defining Project Objectives and Scope

Defining project objectives is the process of clearly identifying and articulating the goals that the project aims to achieve. These objectives serve as the guiding force throughout the project's lifecycle, providing a sense of direction and purpose. The SMART acronym stands for specified, measurable, achievable, relevant, and time-bound (SMART) project objectives. They should be well-defined and clearly communicate what the project intends to accomplish.

The process of defining project objectives begins by understanding the organization's strategic goals and aligning the project with them. This ensures that the project contributes to the overall success of the organization and helps fulfill its mission. Additionally, project managers need to consider the needs and expectations of stakeholders, including clients, customers, and other key individuals or groups impacted by the project. Engaging stakeholders in the objective-setting process fosters buy-in, collaboration, and a shared understanding of the project's purpose.

Once the organization's goals and stakeholder requirements are considered, project managers translate them into specific and measurable objectives. Each objective should be clear and concise, stating what will be achieved and the desired outcomes. Moreover, objectives should be achievable within the constraints of the project, including resources, time, and budget. Setting realistic objectives ensures that the project team can focus their efforts on attainable goals and enhances motivation and commitment.

In addition to being specific and achievable, project objectives should also be relevant. They should directly address the needs and expectations of stakeholders and align with the strategic priorities of the organization. By ensuring relevance, project managers can demonstrate the value and importance of the project, gaining support and resources from stakeholders.

Lastly, project objectives should be time-bound, meaning they have a defined timeline or deadline for completion. The time frame for achieving the objectives helps establish a sense of urgency and enables effective planning and scheduling. A well-defined timeline allows for better resource allocation, task sequencing, and monitoring of progress towards the objectives.

Defining project objectives is a critical step in project management. Clear and well-defined objectives provide a sense of direction, purpose, and focus for the project team. By aligning project objectives with the organization's strategic goals, addressing stakeholder needs, and ensuring they are SMART, project managers set the stage for successful project execution and the achievement of desired outcomes.

1.2 Conducting Feasibility Studies and Risk Assessments

Conducting feasibility studies and risk assessments are essential steps in project management that help evaluate the viability and potential risks associated with a project. Here's an explanation of each process:

Feasibility Studies: Feasibility studies assess the practicality and viability of a project before it is undertaken. These studies analyze various factors to determine if the project is technically, economically, and operationally feasible. The primary objective is to identify any potential barriers, challenges, or limitations that may impact the successful execution and outcome of the project.

During a feasibility study, project managers evaluate multiple aspects such as technical feasibility (e.g., available technology, required expertise), financial feasibility (e.g., cost estimation, return on investment), operational feasibility (e.g., resources, infrastructure), and legal or regulatory compliance. By thoroughly examining these factors, project managers can determine if the project aligns with the organization's capabilities and strategic objectives.

Feasibility studies provide critical insights into the project's potential risks, benefits, and overall viability. They enable stakeholders to make informed decisions about whether to proceed with the project, modify certain aspects, or abandon it altogether. Additionally, feasibility studies help in identifying potential adjustments or refinements that can enhance the project's chances of success.

Risk Assessments: Risk assessments are systematic processes that identify, analyze, and evaluate potential risks associated with a project. Risks are uncertainties or events that can impact the project's objectives, timelines, budget, or overall success. By conducting a thorough risk assessment, project managers can proactively identify and mitigate potential risks to minimize their impact on the project.

The risk assessment process involves identifying and documenting potential risks, assessing their likelihood of occurrence, and evaluating their potential impact on the project. Risks can arise from various sources, such as technical challenges, resource constraints, external dependencies, market volatility, or regulatory changes. Project managers prioritize risks based on their potential severity and develop risk response strategies accordingly.

Risk assessments also involve analyzing the effectiveness of existing risk mitigation measures and identifying additional risk management strategies. Risk acceptance, risk transfer, risk mitigation, and risk avoidance are some of these tactics. By implementing appropriate risk management strategies, project managers enhance the project's resilience and improve the chances of achieving its objectives within the defined constraints.

Overall, conducting feasibility studies and risk assessments are crucial processes in project management. Feasibility studies help determine the practicality and viability of a project, considering various factors that may impact its success. Risk assessments, on the other hand, identify and analyze potential risks associated with the project, enabling project managers to develop effective risk management strategies. By undertaking these assessments, project managers can make informed decisions, mitigate risks, and increase the likelihood of successful project outcomes.

1.3 Stakeholder Identification and Engagement

Stakeholder identification and engagement are fundamental aspects of project management that involve identifying and involving individuals or groups who have an interest or are affected by the project. Here's an explanation of these processes:

Stakeholder Identification: Stakeholder identification is the process of identifying all individuals, groups, or organizations that have an interest in or may be impacted by the project. It is crucial to have a comprehensive understanding of the stakeholders to ensure their needs, expectations, and concerns are considered throughout the project.

Project managers typically start by identifying key stakeholders, such as project sponsors, clients, customers, and project team members. They then expand the stakeholder list by considering other individuals or groups that may have indirect or secondary interests, such as regulatory bodies, suppliers, local communities, or government agencies. Stakeholder identification can be done through various methods, including stakeholder analysis, interviews, surveys, and stakeholder mapping techniques.

Stakeholder Engagement: Stakeholder engagement involves actively involving stakeholders throughout the project lifecycle. It is important to establish open and transparent communication channels to foster collaboration, manage expectations, and gather valuable input from stakeholders. Effective stakeholder engagement helps build support, minimize resistance, and ensure the project's success.

Project managers engage stakeholders by providing regular updates on project progress, milestones, and any changes or decisions that may affect them. They seek feedback, address concerns, and involve stakeholders in decision-making processes when appropriate. Engaging stakeholders early on and involving them in project planning and decision-making increases their sense of ownership and commitment to the project.

Different stakeholders may require different levels and modes of engagement. Some stakeholders may require frequent and detailed communication, while others may prefer periodic updates. Project managers tailor their communication and engagement strategies to suit the needs and preferences of each stakeholder, ensuring that they feel valued and heard.

Stakeholder engagement also involves managing conflicts and resolving issues that may arise during the project. Project managers address conflicts through effective communication, negotiation, and compromise, seeking win-win solutions whenever possible. By actively managing stakeholder relationships, project managers can build trust, maintain support, and mitigate potential risks associated with stakeholder dissatisfaction or resistance.

Stakeholder identification and engagement are integral to successful project management. By identifying and involving stakeholders, project managers ensure that their needs, expectations, and concerns are considered throughout the project. Effective stakeholder engagement enhances collaboration, minimizes resistance, and maximizes stakeholder support, ultimately increasing the chances of project success.

CHAPTER 2

PROJECT PLANNING

Project planning is a crucial phase in the project management lifecycle, where project objectives are defined, project scope is determined, and detailed plans are created to guide project execution. It involves identifying project activities, estimating resources, developing schedules, and establishing a framework for successful project delivery. Here's an overview of the project planning process:

Create a Work Breakdown Structure (WBS):

Break down the project deliverables and activities into smaller, manageable components.

Organize these components in a hierarchical structure using a Work Breakdown Structure (WBS).

Identify Project Activities:

Identify the specific tasks and activities required to complete the project.

Consider dependencies between activities and their sequencing.

Estimate Activity Durations:

Calculate how long you think it will take you to finish each task.

Consult subject matter experts, historical data, and similar projects to make informed duration estimates.

Determine Resource Requirements:

Identify the resources (e.g., human resources, equipment, materials) needed for each activity.

Estimate the quantities and types of resources required.

Develop a Project Schedule:

Use the activity durations, resource availability, and dependencies to create a project schedule.

Represent the schedule visually, using tools like Gantt charts or project management software.

Assess and Mitigate Risks:

Identify potential risks that may impact the project's success.

Develop a risk management plan, including risk identification, analysis, and response strategies.

Allocate and Manage Resources:

Assign resources to activities based on their availability, skills, and requirements.

Continuously monitor and manage resource allocation to ensure efficiency and prevent over allocation.

Develop a Communication Plan:

Define how project information will be communicated to stakeholders.

Determine the frequency, format, and channels of communication.

Establish Project Control Mechanisms:

Define processes for monitoring and controlling the project.

Set up performance metrics, reporting structures, and change control procedures.

Create a Budget:

Develop a detailed budget, including cost estimates for resources, materials, and other project expenses.

Throughout the project lifecycle, keep track of and control project expenditures.

Engage Stakeholders:

Determine the project's stakeholders and their respective duties.

Develop a stakeholder engagement plan to ensure effective communication and involvement.

Obtain Approvals:

Review the project plan with key stakeholders and obtain their approval.

Seek necessary authorizations to proceed with the project.

Project planning provides a roadmap for successful project execution by establishing clear objectives, defining activities, allocating resources, and identifying potential risks. It allows project managers to anticipate challenges, make informed decisions, and effectively manage project constraints. A well-developed project plan sets the foundation for a structured and organized approach to project execution.

2.1 Developing a Project Plan: Deliverables, Milestones, and Timelines

Developing a project plan is a crucial step in project management that involves creating a roadmap for the project's execution. A project plan outlines the project's deliverables, milestones, and timelines. Here's an explanation of each component:

Deliverables: Deliverables are the tangible or intangible outcomes that the project aims to produce or achieve. They are specific and measurable results that contribute to the project's objectives. Project managers work closely with stakeholders to identify and define the deliverables, ensuring that they align with the project's scope and goals.

Deliverables can vary depending on the nature of the project. They can include physical products, completed documents or reports, implemented systems or processes, or achieved milestones. Defining clear deliverables helps set expectations, measure progress, and evaluate the success of the project upon completion.

Milestones: Milestones are significant points or events that mark key stages or achievements in the project. They serve as important indicators of progress and help project teams stay on track. Milestones are typically associated with specific deliverables or significant project tasks.

Project managers identify and define milestones based on the project's timeline and critical objectives. They establish clear criteria and timelines for reaching each milestone, allowing project teams to monitor progress and make necessary adjustments. Milestones also provide opportunities for project stakeholders to review and provide feedback on the project's direction and outputs.

Timelines: Timelines specify the planned sequence and duration of activities or tasks within the project. They outline when each task or deliverable is expected to start and finish, helping project teams understand the project's schedule and resource requirements.

Developing timelines involves breaking down the project into smaller, manageable tasks and estimating the time required to complete each task. Project managers consider dependencies between tasks, resource availability, and any potential risks or constraints that may affect the project's timeline. They create a comprehensive timeline that outlines the project's start date, key milestones, and final delivery date.

Timelines provide project teams with a structured schedule, ensuring that tasks are executed in a logical sequence and deadlines are met. They help in resource planning, task prioritization, and monitoring progress against planned timelines. Timelines are also valuable for stakeholders, as they provide visibility into the project's timeline and allow for effective coordination and communication.

In conclusion, developing a project plan involves defining deliverables, milestones, and timelines. Clear identification of project deliverables helps set objectives and evaluate project success. Milestones mark significant achievements and provide progress indicators throughout the project. Timelines ensure tasks are completed in a timely manner and enable effective scheduling and resource management.

2.2 Resource Allocation and Budgeting

Resource allocation and budgeting are crucial components of project management that involve effectively managing and allocating resources, both in terms of personnel and financial resources. Here's an explanation of each aspect:

Resource Allocation: Resource allocation refers to the process of assigning and distributing resources to different project activities based on their requirements and priorities. This includes allocating human resources, equipment, materials, and any other necessary resources to ensure the successful execution of the project.

Project managers assess the resource needs of each project activity and determine the quantity, skills, and expertise required. They consider the availability of resources, both internal and external, and make informed decisions on how to best allocate them. Resource allocation involves optimizing the utilization of resources, avoiding bottlenecks or overloading, and ensuring that resources are assigned to the right tasks at the right time.

Effective resource allocation helps maximize productivity, minimize delays, and ensure that project activities are completed efficiently. It requires careful planning, coordination, and continuous monitoring to address any resource constraints or changes that may arise during the project's lifecycle.

Budgeting: Budgeting involves estimating, allocating, and controlling the financial resources required for the project. It is the process of developing a detailed budget that outlines the anticipated costs and expenses associated with project activities.

Project managers work closely with stakeholders and financial experts to develop a comprehensive budget that covers all project-related costs, including labor, materials, equipment, subcontractors, and any other direct or indirect expenses. They consider the project's scope, deliverables, timeline, and resource requirements to accurately estimate the costs involved.

Budgeting also involves monitoring and controlling project expenditures to ensure they remain within the allocated budget. Project managers track actual expenses against the budgeted amounts, identify any variances, and take necessary corrective actions to keep the project financially on track. Effective budget management helps prevent cost overruns, optimize resource utilization, and ensure the project's financial viability.

Moreover, project managers need to communicate and report on the budget status to stakeholders, providing transparency and accountability. Regular budget updates and financial reports facilitate informed decision-making and enable stakeholders to understand the financial implications and progress of the project.

Resource allocation and budgeting are integral aspects of project management. Effective resource allocation ensures that the right resources are assigned to the right tasks at the right time, optimizing productivity and minimizing delays. Budgeting involves estimating and controlling project costs, facilitating financial planning and accountability. By managing resources and budget effectively, project managers can enhance project efficiency, mitigate financial risks, and contribute to the overall success of the project.

2.3 Creating a Communication and Reporting Strategy

Creating a communication and reporting strategy is essential in project management to ensure effective and timely exchange of information among project stakeholders. A well-defined strategy facilitates clear and transparent communication, fosters collaboration, and keeps stakeholders informed about project progress. Here's an explanation of key steps involved in creating a communication and reporting strategy:

Identify Stakeholder Communication Needs: Start by identifying the communication needs of various stakeholders involved in the project. Understand their preferences, expectations, and information requirements. Different stakeholders may have different levels of involvement and may require tailored communication approaches. Determine the frequency, format, and channels of communication that will best serve their needs.

Define Communication Channels: Consider the most appropriate communication channels for sharing project information with stakeholders. This could include regular team meetings, email updates, project management software, collaborative platforms, or specific reporting templates. Choose channels that are accessible, convenient, and align with the stakeholders' preferences. Be mindful of the need for both formal and informal communication methods to foster open and transparent exchange of information.

Establish Communication Protocols: Define clear guidelines and protocols for communication within the project team and with external stakeholders. Establish standards for responsiveness, clarity, and professionalism. Clearly communicate expectations regarding communication frequency, decision-making processes, and escalation procedures. This helps ensure consistent and effective communication throughout the project.

Develop Reporting Mechanisms: Determine the reporting requirements and frequency for sharing project progress, milestones, and any significant updates. Establish reporting templates or formats that provide relevant and concise information. Ensure that reports align with stakeholder needs and highlight key project metrics, risks, and achievements. Reporting should be timely, accurate, and concise, focusing on the most critical information for stakeholders to make informed decisions.

Engage in Two-Way Communication: Promote interactive and two-way communication by encouraging stakeholders to provide feedback, ask questions, and express concerns. Create mechanisms for collecting feedback, such as surveys, feedback sessions, or regular check-ins. Actively listen to stakeholder input, address their concerns, and incorporate their feedback into decision-making processes. This fosters engagement, trust, and a collaborative project environment.

Adapt Communication to Stakeholder Preferences: Tailor communication approaches to the specific needs and preferences of different stakeholders. Some stakeholders may prefer more detailed and formal reports, while others may prefer concise summaries or visual representations of data. Adjust the communication style, level of detail, and frequency based on stakeholder requirements. This ensures that information is delivered in a manner that is most effective and meaningful to each stakeholder group.

Monitor and Evaluate Communication Effectiveness: Continuously monitor the effectiveness of the communication and reporting strategy. Seek feedback from stakeholders on the clarity, timeliness, and usefulness of the communication channels and reports. Use this feedback to make improvements and adjustments as necessary. Regularly evaluate the impact of the communication strategy on stakeholder engagement, collaboration, and overall project success.

In conclusion, creating a communication and reporting strategy is crucial for effective project management. By identifying stakeholder communication needs, establishing clear channels and protocols, and engaging in two-way communication, project managers can ensure that stakeholders are well-informed, engaged, and supportive throughout the project. Regular monitoring and evaluation of the communication strategy help maintain its effectiveness and adapt it to evolving stakeholder requirements.

CHAPTER 3

TEAM MANAGEMENT AND LEADERSHIP

Team management and leadership are critical aspects of project management that involve guiding, motivating, and effectively managing a project team to achieve project objectives. Successful team management and leadership contribute to a positive team culture, enhanced collaboration, and improved project outcomes. Here are key considerations for team management and leadership in project management:

Team Building:

Create a cohesive project team by fostering a sense of camaraderie, trust, and mutual respect.

Encourage open communication, active listening, and collaboration among team members.

Foster a supportive and inclusive team culture that values diversity and encourages different perspectives.

Clear Roles and Responsibilities:

Define clear roles and responsibilities for each team member to ensure accountability and clarity.

Clearly communicate expectations, deliverables, and timelines to avoid misunderstandings.

Effective Communication:

Establish open and transparent communication channels to facilitate effective information sharing.

Foster a culture of active and respectful communication, where team members feel comfortable expressing their ideas and concerns.

Utilize various communication methods, such as meetings, emails, project management tools, and collaborative platforms.

Leadership:

Provide strong project leadership by setting a clear vision, direction, and goals for the team.

Inspire and motivate team members to achieve their best performance and encourage professional growth.

Lead by example, demonstrating professionalism, integrity, and a positive attitude.

Conflict Resolution:

Anticipate and address conflicts among team members promptly and constructively.

Encourage open dialogue to understand different perspectives and facilitate resolution.

Implement conflict resolution strategies that focus on collaboration and finding win-win solutions.

Empowerment and Delegation:

Delegate tasks and responsibilities to team members based on their skills and capabilities.

Empower team members to make decisions and take ownership of their work.

Provide guidance and support when needed, but also allow autonomy and opportunities for growth.

Continuous Development:

Support the professional development of team members through training, coaching, and mentorship.

Encourage a learning culture where team members can enhance their skills and knowledge.

Provide opportunities for team members to work on challenging assignments and expand their capabilities.

Recognition and Rewards:

Recognize and appreciate the efforts and achievements of team members.

Provide timely feedback and constructive criticism to help team members improve.

Consider implementing rewards and incentives to motivate and reinforce positive performance.

Performance Management:

Regularly evaluate team and individual performance against project goals and objectives.

Provide feedback on performance and identify areas for improvement.

Implement performance improvement plans when necessary to address any performance gaps.

Team Empowerment:

Encourage collaboration, innovation, and creativity within the team.

Create an environment where team members feel empowered to contribute ideas and take initiative.

Support autonomy and trust team members to make decisions within their areas of responsibility.

Effective team management and leadership are crucial for maximizing the potential of a project team and driving project success. By fostering a positive team culture, promoting open communication, and providing strong leadership, project managers can create a motivated and engaged team that performs at its best and delivers outstanding results.

3.1 Building a High-Performing Project Team

Building a high-performing project team is vital for project success. A cohesive and motivated team can maximize productivity, overcome challenges, and deliver outstanding results. Here are key steps to consider when building a high-performing project team:

Define tasks and Responsibilities: Clearly outline each team member's tasks and responsibilities. Ensure that team members understand their individual contributions to the project and how their roles fit into the overall project objectives. This clarity helps minimize confusion, establishes accountability, and promotes effective collaboration.

Recruit and Select Team Members Carefully: Take a thoughtful approach when selecting team members. Look for individuals who possess the necessary skills, expertise, and experience relevant to the project requirements. Assess their ability to work well in a team, communicate effectively, and handle project challenges. Strive for diversity in skills, backgrounds, and perspectives to foster innovation and adaptability.

Foster a Positive Team Culture: Create an environment that promotes trust, respect, and open communication. Encourage collaboration, active participation, and sharing of ideas and knowledge among team members. Foster a sense of camaraderie, where team members support and rely on each other. Celebrate achievements, recognize contributions, and create opportunities for team-building activities.

Provide Clear Goals and Expectations: Clearly communicate project goals, deliverables, and performance expectations to the team. Establish measurable objectives and milestones to track progress. Ensure that team members have a clear understanding of what success looks like and how their individual contributions align with the project's overall objectives.

Encourage Continuous Learning and Development: Support the professional growth of team members by providing opportunities for training, skill development, and knowledge sharing. Encourage individuals to expand their expertise and stay updated on industry trends and best practices. Foster a learning culture where team members are motivated to enhance their skills and bring new ideas to the project.

Promote Effective Communication: Establish channels for open and transparent communication within the team. Encourage regular status updates, progress reporting, and sharing of information. Foster a culture where team members feel comfortable expressing concerns, asking questions, and providing constructive feedback. Facilitate effective communication between team members, stakeholders, and project sponsors.

Empower and Delegate: Delegate tasks and responsibilities based on individual strengths and expertise. Provide team members with autonomy and decision-making authority within their assigned roles. Empower team members to take ownership of their work, encourage innovation, and provide them with the necessary support and resources to succeed.

Address Conflict Promptly: Conflict can arise within any team. Address conflicts promptly and effectively to maintain a harmonious working environment. Encourage open and honest discussions to resolve differences and find mutually beneficial solutions. Provide a supportive framework for conflict resolution and ensure that all team members feel heard and respected.

Regularly Monitor and Provide Feedback: Continuously monitor team performance and provide constructive feedback. Offer recognition for accomplishments and provide guidance for improvement when needed. Regularly assess the team's progress, identify areas for enhancement, and make necessary adjustments to keep the team on track.

Foster a Positive Work-Life Balance: Recognize the importance of work-life balance and encourage team members to maintain a healthy equilibrium. Support flexible working arrangements, promote time management techniques, and encourage well-being practices within the team.

In conclusion, building a high-performing project team requires a combination of clear communication, fostering a positive team culture, providing support for professional growth, and effective collaboration. By carefully selecting team members, establishing clear goals and expectations, and nurturing a supportive work environment, project managers can create a team that excels in delivering successful outcomes.

3.2 Effective Communication and Collaboration

Collaboration and effective communication are crucial for successful project management. They enable team members to work together efficiently, share information, resolve conflicts, and achieve project goals. Here's an explanation of these two key aspects:

Effective Communication:

Effective communication is the foundation of successful project management. It involves the exchange of information, ideas, feedback, and instructions among project team members, stakeholders, and sponsors. Following are some essential guidelines for good communication:

a. Clear and Concise: Communication should be clear, concise, and easily understood by all recipients. Use simple language, avoid jargon or technical terms, and ensure that the intended message is accurately conveyed.

b. Active Listening: Listening actively is crucial to understanding others' perspectives and ensuring effective communication. Give full attention to the speaker, ask questions for clarification, and show empathy and understanding.

c. Open and Transparent: Encourage an open and transparent communication culture where team members feel comfortable expressing their thoughts, concerns, and ideas. Foster an environment where constructive feedback is welcomed and valued.

d. Use Various Communication Channels: Utilize a mix of communication channels, such as face-to-face meetings, emails, project management tools, collaborative platforms, and video conferences. Choose the appropriate channel based on the nature of the message and the preferences of the recipients.

e. Regular Updates: Provide regular project updates to keep stakeholders informed about the project's progress, achievements, and any changes or challenges. Ensure that stakeholders are aware of milestones, deadlines, and potential impacts on project delivery.

f. Tailored Communication: Recognize that different stakeholders have different information needs and communication preferences. Customize your communication approach to meet the specific requirements of each stakeholder group, ensuring that the information shared is relevant and meaningful to them.

Collaboration:

Collaboration is the process of working together as a team to achieve project objectives. It involves pooling resources, knowledge, and skills to enhance problem-solving, decision-making, and innovation. Here are some key principles of effective collaboration:

a. **Teamwork:** Foster a collaborative and supportive team environment where individuals work together towards a common goal. Encourage cooperation, active participation, and a shared sense of responsibility.

b. **Clear Roles and Responsibilities:** Clearly define and communicate the roles and responsibilities of each team member. Ensure that everyone understands their contributions to the project and how their work aligns with the overall objectives.

c. **Trust and Respect:** Build trust and mutual respect among team members. Foster an environment where ideas are valued, diverse opinions are encouraged, and constructive feedback is provided. Trust allows for open and honest communication and promotes effective collaboration.

d. **Encourage Knowledge Sharing:** Promote knowledge sharing and learning within the team. Team members should be encouraged to share their knowledge, best practices, and lessons gained. Establish mechanisms for capturing and disseminating knowledge throughout the project.

e. **Effective Conflict Resolution:** Conflict is inevitable in any collaborative environment. Encourage open and constructive discussions to address conflicts and differences of opinion. Foster a problem-solving approach to conflict resolution, seeking win-win solutions that benefit the project and maintain positive working relationships.

f. **Regular Collaboration Activities:** Foster collaboration through regular team meetings, brainstorming sessions, workshops, and collaborative tools. Create opportunities for cross-functional collaboration, where team members from different disciplines or departments can work together on shared challenges.

By prioritizing effective communication and collaboration, project managers can foster a cohesive and productive team. This not only improves project outcomes but also creates a positive working environment that enhances team morale and satisfaction.

3.3 Motivating and Engaging Team Members

Motivating and engaging team members is vital for maximizing their productivity, fostering collaboration, and achieving project success. Here are some strategies to effectively motivate and engage your project team:

Clearly Communicate Project Goals: Ensure that team members have a clear understanding of the project goals, objectives, and their role in achieving them. Explain how their contributions align with the project's overall vision and the impact they can make. When team members see the bigger picture and understand the purpose of their work, they are more motivated to perform at their best.

Provide Autonomy and Ownership: Empower team members by giving them autonomy and ownership over their work. Encourage them to take responsibility for their tasks, make decisions, and contribute their ideas and expertise. When individuals feel a sense of ownership and control over their work, they are more likely to be engaged and motivated.

Recognize and Celebrate Achievements: Acknowledge and appreciate the efforts and achievements of team members. Regularly recognize their contributions and celebrate milestones or successful project outcomes. This can be done through verbal praise, written acknowledgments, team celebrations, or rewards. Recognizing and rewarding individual and team accomplishments boosts morale and motivates team members to continue performing at a high level.

Foster a Positive Work Environment: Create a positive work environment that promotes trust, respect, and open communication. Encourage team members to work together, exchange ideas, and support one another. Foster a culture where everyone feels valued, included, and heard. A positive work environment enhances team satisfaction, engagement, and motivation.

Provide Opportunities for Growth and Development: Offer opportunities for team members to enhance their skills, acquire new knowledge, and grow professionally. Support their professional development through training programs, workshops, mentorship, or access to resources. When team members see opportunities for personal and professional growth, they are more likely to be engaged and motivated.

Encourage Collaboration and Teamwork: Foster a collaborative and inclusive team culture. Encourage teamwork, collaboration, and knowledge sharing. Create opportunities for team members to work together, exchange ideas, and learn from one another. Collaboration strengthens team bonds, encourages creativity, and boosts overall team morale.

Set Realistic and Challenging Goals: Establish clear and achievable goals that challenge team members to stretch their abilities and skills. Ensure that goals are realistic and aligned with the team's capabilities and available resources. When team members are engaged in meaningful and challenging work, they are more likely to be motivated and committed to achieving success.

Provide Regular Feedback and Support: Offer ongoing feedback and support to team members. Provide constructive feedback on their performance, highlighting strengths and areas for improvement. Offer guidance and assistance when needed. Regular check-ins and open communication channels allow team members to seek help, clarify expectations, and address any concerns promptly.

Encourage Work-Life Balance: Promote a healthy work-life balance among team members. Encourage them to take breaks, manage their workload, and prioritize self-care. Recognize the importance of a well-balanced life, as it contributes to overall well-being and sustained motivation.

Lead by Example: As a project manager, lead by example and exhibit the qualities you expect from your team members. Demonstrate a strong work ethic, positive attitude, and commitment to the project. Your staff will be inspired and motivated by your enthusiasm and commitment.

Remember that each team member may have different motivators and preferences. Take the time to understand their individual needs and adjust your motivational strategies accordingly. By effectively motivating and engaging your team members, you create an environment that fosters high performance, collaboration, and project success.

CHAPTER 4

RISK MANAGEMENT

In the dynamic landscape of project management, risk is an ever-present companion that can either propel us towards success or drag us into failure. Projects, by their nature, are laden with uncertainties, complexities, and unexpected challenges. A meticulous approach to risk management is crucial to navigate these treacherous waters and ensure project success. This article explores the profound importance of risk management in project execution, highlighting its key principles, methodologies, and the transformative impact it can have on project outcomes.

Understanding the Essence of Risk Management:

Risk management is not merely about identifying potential threats and mitigating their impact; it is a comprehensive framework that encompasses proactive strategies to assess, analyze, respond to, and monitor risks throughout the project lifecycle. It involves a systematic approach to anticipate, understand, and mitigate uncertainties that could hinder project objectives, schedules, costs, or quality.

The Role of Risk Management in Project Success:

Effective risk management serves as the cornerstone of project success. It enables project managers to:

a. **Anticipate and Mitigate Potential Threats:** By proactively identifying and assessing risks, project teams gain valuable insights into potential stumbling blocks. This knowledge empowers them to develop contingency plans and implement preventive measures to mitigate these risks, thereby minimizing their impact on project outcomes.

b. **Enhance Decision-making:** Risk management facilitates informed decision-making by providing stakeholders with a clear understanding of the potential risks associated with various options. By evaluating risks alongside potential rewards, project teams can make well-informed choices that optimize project success.

c. **Improve Resource Allocation:** Risk management helps in identifying critical areas where resources should be allocated to minimize potential threats. It ensures that resources are strategically utilized, focusing on areas that pose the greatest risks to the project's success.

d. **Foster Stakeholder Confidence:** A robust risk management process demonstrates the project team's commitment to transparency and accountability. By actively involving stakeholders in risk assessment and mitigation activities, trust is built, and confidence in project success is fostered.

Key Principles of Risk Management:

a. **Risk Identification:** Thoroughly analyze the project environment, considering internal and external factors, to identify potential risks that could impact project objectives.

b. **Risk Assessment:** Evaluate the probability and potential impact of each identified risk, prioritizing them based on severity and likelihood.

c. Risk Response Planning: Develop appropriate response strategies for each identified risk, including contingency plans, preventive measures, or risk transfer options.

d. Risk Monitoring and Control: Continuously monitor the project's risk landscape, ensuring that risk response plans are implemented effectively and adjusting strategies as needed.

e. Continuous Learning: Encourage a culture of learning from past projects, both successful and unsuccessful, to refine risk management processes and enhance future project outcomes.

Effective Risk Management Methodologies:

a. Qualitative Risk Analysis: Assess risks based on their probability and impact using techniques such as risk probability and impact assessment, risk matrix, or risk categorization.

b. Quantitative Risk Analysis: Utilize statistical models, simulations, or Monte Carlo analysis to assign numerical values to risks, enabling a more precise understanding of their potential impact on project objectives.

c. Risk Response Strategies: Employ appropriate strategies such as risk avoidance, risk transfer, risk mitigation, or risk acceptance to manage identified risks effectively.

d. Risk Monitoring and Control Tools: Utilize project management software, risk registers, and key performance indicators to monitor and track risks throughout the project lifecycle, ensuring timely response and adjustment when necessary.

Risk management is not a luxury but a necessity in the realm of project management. It empowers project teams to proactively navigate uncertainty, safeguard project success, and deliver exceptional outcomes. By adopting a comprehensive risk management approach, project managers can minimize potential threats, enhance decision-making, allocate resources effectively, and foster stakeholder confidence. With risk management at the core of project execution, organizations can embrace challenges, seize opportunities, and steer their projects towards excellence in a constantly evolving business landscape.

4.1 Identifying and Assessing Project Risks

Identifying and assessing project risks is a crucial step in project management. It helps project managers and teams anticipate potential problems or obstacles that may arise during the project's lifecycle. Here are some steps to effectively identify and assess project risks:

Gather a project team: Bring together a diverse group of individuals with relevant expertise and perspectives. This can include project managers, team members, stakeholders, and subject matter experts.

Brainstorm potential risks: Conduct a brainstorming session to generate a list of potential risks. Encourage participants to think broadly and consider various aspects of the project, such as scope, schedule, resources, technology, external factors, and dependencies.

Categorize risks: Group similar risks together based on their nature or cause. Common categories include technical risks, organizational risks, financial risks, schedule risks, and external risks. This helps in organizing and prioritizing risks during the assessment phase.

Assess risks: Evaluate the identified risks based on their likelihood of occurrence and potential impact on the project objectives. This assessment can be qualitative (low, medium, high) or quantitative (using specific metrics or probability calculations). Consider the potential consequences, such as cost overruns, schedule delays, quality issues, or stakeholder dissatisfaction.

Prioritize risks: Prioritize the risks based on their assessed significance. Focus on risks with high likelihood and high impact first, as they pose the greatest threat to project success. You can then allocate resources and create suitable risk mitigation methods as a result.

Analyze root causes: Identify the root causes or triggers of each risk. Understanding the underlying factors helps in developing effective risk response strategies and preventive measures. It also aids in addressing the source of the risk rather than just treating the symptoms.

Develop risk response strategies: For each prioritized risk, determine appropriate response strategies. These can include risk avoidance (eliminating the risk altogether), risk mitigation (reducing the likelihood or impact), risk transfer (shifting the risk to another party through contracts or insurance), or risk acceptance (acknowledging the risk and having a contingency plan).

Create a risk management plan: Consolidate all the identified risks, assessments, prioritization, and response strategies into a comprehensive risk management plan. The plan should outline the responsibilities, communication channels, monitoring and control mechanisms, and contingency plans to address the identified risks throughout the project.

Monitor and control risks: Regularly monitor the identified risks throughout the project's lifecycle. Keep track of their status, reassess their likelihood and impact if necessary, and implement the planned risk response strategies. Communicate any changes or updates to the project team and stakeholders.

Learn from experience: After the project is completed, review the effectiveness of the risk management strategies employed. Determine what needs to be improved, best practices, and lessons learned. Document these insights to enhance future risk identification and assessment processes.

Remember, risk management is an iterative process, and risks should be continuously monitored and managed throughout the project. By proactively identifying and assessing project risks, you increase the chances of successfully navigating challenges and achieving project objectives.

4.2 Mitigation and Contingency Planning

Mitigation and contingency planning are essential components of effective risk management in projects. They involve developing strategies and actions to reduce the impact of identified risks and to respond effectively if those risks materialize. Here's how you can approach mitigation and contingency planning:

Risk Mitigation:

Identify specific actions: Based on the identified risks, determine specific actions that can be taken to reduce the likelihood or impact of each risk. These actions should address the root causes or triggers of the risk.

Develop preventive measures: Implement measures to proactively prevent the occurrence of risks or to minimize their potential consequences. This may involve strengthening project processes, enhancing quality control, providing additional training, or improving communication channels.

Allocate resources: Determine the necessary resources, such as budget, time, personnel, or technology, required to implement the risk mitigation actions effectively.

Assign responsibilities: Clearly assign responsibilities to team members or stakeholders who will be accountable for implementing the risk mitigation measures. Ensure that they have the necessary authority and resources to carry out their tasks.

Contingency Planning:

Identify potential scenarios: Consider the risks that have a higher likelihood of occurring or a significant potential impact. Identify potential scenarios or situations that could arise if those risks materialize.

Determine response strategies: Develop response strategies or actions that can be activated if the identified risks actually occur. These strategies should outline what steps to take to mitigate the consequences and address the situation.

Establish triggers: Define specific triggers or indicators that will prompt the activation of contingency plans. Triggers can be certain events, metrics, or thresholds that signal the occurrence or likelihood of a risk.

Define communication and decision-making processes: Clearly define how the project team will communicate, make decisions, and execute the contingency plans. Establish clear communication channels and roles so that everyone knows their responsibilities and can act swiftly if needed.

Prepare alternative approaches: Consider alternative approaches or workarounds that can be implemented if a risk materializes. These alternatives should be developed in advance to minimize disruption and keep the project on track.

Allocate resources: Determine the necessary resources, such as additional budget, time, or personnel, required to implement the contingency plans effectively. Ensure that these resources are readily available if needed.

Test and review: Periodically test the contingency plans to ensure their effectiveness and feasibility. Review and update them as needed based on lessons learned from past experiences or changes in project circumstances.

By proactively engaging in risk mitigation and contingency planning, you increase the project's resilience and reduce the negative impacts of risks. These strategies help you address potential problems before they occur or respond efficiently when they do, enhancing the overall project success.

4.3 Monitoring and Controlling Project Risks

Monitoring and controlling project risks is crucial to ensure that risk management efforts remain effective throughout the project's lifecycle. It involves actively tracking identified risks, assessing their status, and implementing appropriate actions to keep them within acceptable boundaries. Here's how you can approach monitoring and controlling project risks:

Establish a Risk Management Plan: Begin by developing a comprehensive risk management plan that outlines the overall approach to risk monitoring and control. Define roles and responsibilities, communication channels, monitoring methods, and reporting mechanisms.

Regular Risk Assessments: Conduct regular risk assessments to evaluate the status of identified risks. Reassess the likelihood and impact of risks, considering any changes in project circumstances, new information, or emerging risks. This helps in prioritizing risks and determining the need for additional mitigation or contingency actions.

Monitoring Mechanisms: Implement monitoring mechanisms to track the identified risks. This can include regular progress updates, status meetings, performance indicators, checklists, or automated tools. Ensure that these mechanisms capture relevant data and provide timely information on the status of risks.

Risk Triggers: Define triggers or early warning signs that indicate a risk is escalating or approaching a critical threshold. These triggers can be quantitative or qualitative indicators that prompt immediate attention and action. Establish clear protocols for responding to risk triggers, including communication and escalation procedures.

Communication and Reporting: Maintain effective communication channels to share risk-related information with the project team, stakeholders, and decision-makers. Regularly report on the status of identified risks, progress in risk mitigation, and any changes in risk profiles. Tailor the communication to different stakeholders, providing the level of detail and frequency that suits their needs.

Risk Response Actions: Implement the planned risk response actions as outlined in the risk management plan. Ensure that the assigned responsibilities are fulfilled, and actions are taken within the designated timeframes. Monitor the effectiveness of risk response actions and make adjustments as necessary.

Contingency Activation: Activate contingency plans when triggered by predefined events or risk occurrences. Promptly execute the contingency actions to minimize the impact of risks that have materialized. Monitor the effectiveness of the contingency plans and adjust them if needed.

Documentation and Lessons Learned: Maintain proper documentation of risk monitoring and control activities. This includes recording risk assessments, mitigation actions taken, contingency activations, and outcomes. Capture lessons learned from risk events and incorporate them into future risk management practices.

Stakeholder Engagement: Engage relevant stakeholders in the risk monitoring and control processes. Seek their input, insights, and feedback to enhance risk awareness and facilitate informed decision-making. Address any concerns or suggestions raised by stakeholders promptly.

Continuous Improvement: Continuously evaluate the effectiveness of the risk monitoring and control processes. Identify areas for improvement and implement necessary adjustments in risk management strategies, tools, or approaches. Apply lessons learned from previous projects to enhance future risk management practices.

By diligently monitoring and controlling project risks, you can identify potential issues early, take timely actions, and maintain project objectives within acceptable risk tolerances. This proactive approach contributes to successful project outcomes and minimizes the negative impacts of risks.

CHAPTER 5

PROJECT EXECUTION

Project execution in project management refers to the phase where the planned activities and tasks are implemented to accomplish the project objectives. It involves the coordination of resources, communication, and monitoring of progress to ensure successful project delivery. During this phase, the project team carries out the defined project activities, adheres to the project plan, and manages any changes or issues that arise.

The first step in project execution is to mobilize the project team and allocate the necessary resources, such as human resources, equipment, and materials. The project manager plays a crucial role in guiding and supervising the team, assigning responsibilities, and establishing a clear line of communication. As the project progresses, regular monitoring and control measures are implemented to track the project's progress, identify any deviations from the plan, and take corrective actions as needed. This may involve conducting regular team meetings, reviewing project documentation, and assessing the quality of deliverables. The project manager also ensures effective stakeholder engagement and manages any risks or issues that may arise during the execution phase. Overall, project execution focuses on executing the project plan, managing resources, and maintaining effective communication and control throughout the project lifecycle.

5.1 Implementing the Project Plan

Implementing the project plan involves putting the planned activities into action and executing the project according to the defined scope, schedule, budget, and quality standards. Here are the key steps to effectively implement a project plan:

Assign Responsibilities: Clearly define and communicate the roles and responsibilities of each team member involved in the project. Ensure that everyone understands their tasks, deliverables, and deadlines. Establish a reporting structure and communication channels to facilitate coordination and collaboration.

Create a Work Breakdown Structure (WBS): Develop a WBS to break down the project scope into manageable tasks and subtasks. Organize these tasks in a hierarchical structure to provide a clear overview of the work to be done. Assign resources, estimate durations, and establish dependencies between tasks.

Develop a Project Schedule: Use the WBS to create a project schedule. Define the start and end dates for each task, considering resource availability and dependencies. Allocate resources effectively, taking into account their skills, availability, and workload. Identify critical path activities that directly impact the project's overall timeline.

Allocate Resources: Allocate resources, including personnel, equipment, and materials, to each task based on the project requirements and schedule. Ensure that resources are adequately trained, available when needed, and have the necessary skills and expertise.

Communicate the Project Plan: Share the project plan with the project team, stakeholders, and other relevant parties. Ensure that everyone understands the project objectives, scope, schedule, and expected outcomes. Respond to any queries or issues expressed by stakeholders.

Implement Project Control Measures: Put in place control measures to track project progress, identify deviations from the plan, and take corrective actions. This may involve setting up regular progress meetings, using project management software, or implementing performance tracking mechanisms.

Execute Tasks: Begin executing the project tasks according to the defined schedule. Monitor the progress of each task, track actual effort and costs, and compare them against the planned values. Address any issues or roadblocks that arise promptly.

Manage Changes: As the project progresses, changes may be required due to unforeseen circumstances, stakeholder requests, or new information. Establish a change control process to evaluate change requests, assess their impact on the project, and make informed decisions regarding their implementation.

Monitor Risks: Continuously monitor and manage project risks as per the established risk management plan. Regularly assess the identified risks, implement risk mitigation strategies, and activate contingency plans when necessary. Keep stakeholders informed of any significant risk-related developments.

Ensure Quality Control: Implement quality control measures to ensure that project deliverables meet the defined quality standards. Monitor and evaluate the quality of work being produced, conduct inspections or tests as required, and address any quality issues promptly.

Document Progress: Maintain documentation of project progress, including completed tasks, milestones achieved, changes made, and any issues or challenges encountered. Keep records of communication, decisions, and lessons learned throughout the project.

Monitor Budget: Regularly track project costs against the planned budget. Monitor expenditure on resources, materials, and other project-related expenses. Take corrective actions if the actual costs deviate significantly from the budget.

Manage Stakeholder Engagement: Continuously engage with stakeholders and keep them informed of project progress. Address their concerns, provide regular updates, and seek their feedback. Maintain open lines of communication to ensure their ongoing support and alignment with project goals.

Review and Adjust: Periodically review the project plan, schedule, and performance against the defined objectives. Assess the need for adjustments, considering any changes in project requirements, external factors, or lessons learned. Make necessary modifications to the plan and communicate them to the team and stakeholders.

By following these steps, you can effectively implement a project plan and increase the likelihood of achieving project objectives within the defined constraints of scope, schedule, budget, and quality. Regular monitoring, communication, and adaptation are key to successful project implementation.

5.2 Monitoring Progress and Making Adjustments

Monitoring progress and making adjustments are critical aspects of project management that ensure the project stays on track and aligns with its objectives. Here's a step-by-step approach to effectively monitor progress and make necessary adjustments:

Define Key Performance Indicators (KPIs): Determine the KPIs that will measure the project's progress and success. These indicators should align with the project's objectives, such as completion milestones, deliverable quality, budget adherence, and stakeholder satisfaction.

Establish Monitoring and Reporting Mechanisms: Set up a system to collect data and track progress against the defined KPIs. This can involve regular status updates, progress reports, milestone reviews, or project management software. Determine the frequency and format of reporting to ensure timely and accurate information.

Regularly Monitor Project Activities: Continuously monitor project activities to track progress and identify any deviations from the plan. Keep an eye on task completion, resource utilization, budget expenditure, and adherence to the project schedule. Actively communicate with team members, stakeholders, and sponsors to gather insights and updates.

Analyze Variances and Deviations: Compare actual progress against the planned targets and assess any deviations or variances. Identify the root causes of these variances, such as unexpected obstacles, scope changes, resource constraints, or external factors. Analyze the impact of these variances on the project's objectives, timeline, and budget.

Conduct Performance Reviews: Periodically conduct performance reviews to evaluate the quality and efficiency of project deliverables. This can involve peer reviews, quality assessments, customer feedback, or stakeholder surveys. Assess whether the project is meeting the desired standards and identify areas for improvement.

Identify Risks and Issues: Continuously monitor and assess project risks and issues. Identify any new risks that have emerged or existing risks that require attention. Evaluate the severity, probability, and potential impact of these risks on the project. Address issues promptly to prevent them from escalating and impacting project progress.

Review and Adjust the Project Plan: Based on the insights gained from monitoring, variances, performance reviews, and risk assessments, review the project plan. Determine whether adjustments are necessary to realign the project with its objectives and address any challenges or deviations. This may involve revising the schedule, modifying resource allocation, updating the budget, or changing the scope.

Communicate Adjustments: Communicate any adjustments or changes to the project plan to the project team, stakeholders, and sponsors. Clearly articulate the reasons behind the adjustments and the expected impact on the project. Seek feedback and alignment to ensure everyone understands and supports the revised plan.

Revise Resource Allocation: If adjustments require changes in resource allocation, reallocate resources accordingly. Consider the availability, skills, and workload of team members to ensure they are assigned to the appropriate tasks. Communicate any changes in roles or responsibilities to the team members.

Implement Corrective Actions: Develop and implement corrective actions to address deviations, mitigate risks, and resolve issues. This may involve additional training, process improvements, stakeholder engagement strategies, or resource reallocation. Take prompt action to bring the project back on track and prevent further deviations.

Monitor and Evaluate Adjustments: Continuously monitor the effectiveness of the adjustments made. Assess whether the corrective actions have resulted in the desired outcomes and improvements. Measure progress against the revised plan and KPIs to ensure the project is moving towards its objectives.

Repeat the Monitoring and Adjustment Cycle: Project monitoring and adjustment should be an ongoing process throughout the project's lifecycle. Continuously monitor progress, identify deviations, make necessary adjustments, and repeat the cycle to keep the project aligned with its objectives.

By following these steps, you can effectively monitor project progress, identify areas requiring adjustments, and take timely actions to keep the project on track towards its desiredoutcomes. Regular monitoring and proactive adjustments increase the chances of project success and help mitigate risks and challenges along the way.

5.3 Managing Change and Scope Creep

Managing change and scope creep is crucial to maintain project control and ensure that project objectives are achieved within the defined constraints. Here's a step-by-step approach to effectively manage change and scope creep:

Establish a Change Control Process: Set up a formal change control process that clearly defines how changes to the project scope will be requested, evaluated, approved, and implemented. This process should outline the roles and responsibilities of stakeholders involved in change management.

Clearly Define the Project Scope: Ensure that the project scope is clearly defined and documented from the beginning. This includes the project objectives, deliverables, boundaries, and any exclusions. Clearly communicate the agreed-upon scope to the project team and stakeholders.

Monitor and Identify Changes: Continuously monitor the project for potential changes and scope creep. Actively engage with stakeholders, conduct regular progress reviews, and encourage open communication to identify any emerging needs or requests for scope expansion.

Evaluate Change Requests: When a change request is submitted, evaluate its impact on the project's scope, schedule, resources, and budget. Assess whether the change aligns with the project's objectives and whether it is necessary and feasible.

Assess Implications: Analyze the implications of the change on the project, including its impact on project constraints, risks, and dependencies. Consider the potential effects on the project timeline, resources, budget, and other ongoing activities. Evaluate the trade-offs and potential risks associated with implementing the change.

Prioritize and Make Decisions: Prioritize change requests based on their urgency, importance, and alignment with project objectives. Assess the value-add and potential risks of each change. Involve key stakeholders, including the project sponsor, in decision-making to ensure alignment and consensus.

Communicate and Negotiate: Effectively communicate the decision regarding the change request to all relevant stakeholders. Clearly explain the rationale behind the decision, including any constraints or impacts that influenced the outcome. Engage in negotiation and discussion, if necessary, to reach a mutual understanding and agreement.

Update the Project Plan: If the change is approved, update the project plan to reflect the revised scope, schedule, resources, and budget. Ensure that all project documentation, including the WBS, schedule, and resource allocation, are updated to reflect the changes.

Monitor and Control Scope Creep: Continuously monitor and control scope creep throughout the project. Regularly assess whether the project is deviating from the agreed-upon scope and take corrective actions if needed. Engage in ongoing scope management to prevent uncontrolled expansion.

Educate and Manage Expectations: Proactively manage stakeholder expectations regarding project scope and change management. Educate stakeholders on the impacts of scope changes and the importance of adhering to the agreed-upon scope. Set realistic expectations and communicate the need for controlled change to prevent negative consequences.

Document Changes and Lessons Learned: Maintain thorough documentation of all approved changes, including the rationale, impacts, and outcomes. Use these documented changes as a reference for future projects and to improve change management processes. Capture lessons learned to enhance future scope management and change control efforts.

By following these steps, you can effectively manage change and scope creep, ensuring that the project remains aligned with its objectives while accommodating necessary modifications within the defined constraints.

CHAPTER 6

QUALITY ASSURANCE AND CONTROL

Quality assurance and control are essential components of project management that ensure the project's deliverables and processes meet the defined quality standards. Quality assurance involves the systematic and planned activities conducted throughout the project to prevent defects and verify that the project is being executed according to the established quality criteria. It includes processes such as quality planning, quality audits, and process improvement to proactively address quality issues and ensure that the project meets the desired level of excellence.

On the other hand, quality control focuses on monitoring and inspecting the project's outputs to identify and correct any defects or deviations from the quality standards. It involves measuring the actual project results against the predetermined quality requirements, using techniques such as inspections, tests, and reviews. Quality control activities are performed throughout the project lifecycle, from the initial development stages to the final deliverables, to ensure that the project outputs meet the defined quality standards and the client's expectations. Both quality assurance and control are crucial for maintaining the project's quality, improving overall performance, and enhancing customer satisfaction by delivering high-quality outputs.

6.1 Standard ethics for quality assurance and control

Integrity: Upholding the highest standards of honesty, transparency, and ethical conduct throughout the project management process.

Objectivity: Ensuring that decisions related to quality assurance and control are based on unbiased assessments and objective criteria rather than personal interests or biases.

Professional Competence: Demonstrating expertise and proficiency in quality assurance and control methodologies, tools, and techniques through continuous learning and professional development.

Confidentiality: Respecting the confidentiality of sensitive project information and ensuring that it is appropriately protected from unauthorized access or disclosure.

Independence: Maintaining independence and impartiality in conducting quality assurance and control activities, free from undue influence or conflicts of interest.

Accountability: Taking responsibility for the quality outcomes of the project and being answerable for the decisions made and actions taken during quality assurance and control processes.

Fairness: Treating all stakeholders, team members, and project participants with fairness, respect, and impartiality, without favoritism or discrimination.

Compliance: Adhering to applicable laws, regulations, industry standards, and organizational policies related to quality assurance and control, ensuring that all activities are conducted within legal and ethical boundaries.

Stakeholder Engagement: Engaging stakeholders in quality assurance and control processes, seeking their input, and considering their perspectives to ensure that their needs and expectations are met.

Continuous Improvement: Promoting a culture of continuous improvement by actively seeking opportunities to enhance quality assurance and control processes, incorporating lessons learned, and implementing best practices to deliver optimal project outcomes.

It's important to note that while these ethics provide a general framework for quality assurance and control in project management, specific organizations or professional bodies may have additional or more specific codes of ethics that project managers should adhere to.

6.2 Establishing Quality Standards and Metrics

Establishing quality standards and metrics is essential to ensure that project deliverables meet the desired level of quality. Quality standards define the expectations and criteria for the project's outputs, while metrics provide measurable indicators to assess and monitor the quality throughout the project lifecycle. Here's how you can establish quality standards and metrics:

Define Quality Objectives: Clearly articulate the quality objectives for the project. These objectives should align with the project's overall goals and stakeholder expectations. Consider factors such as functionality, performance, reliability, usability, maintainability, and compliance requirements.

Identify Quality Criteria: Determine the specific criteria or attributes that will be used to evaluate the quality of the project deliverables. For example, this could include accuracy, completeness, consistency, efficiency, adherence to standards or regulations, and customer satisfaction.

Establish Quality Standards: Develop specific quality standards that outline the acceptable level of performance or characteristics for each quality criterion. These standards should be measurable, objective, and achievable. They can be based on industry best practices, regulatory requirements, or internal benchmarks.

Define Quality Metrics: Identify and establish measurable metrics that will be used to assess the quality of project outputs. Select metrics that are relevant to the specific quality criteria and can be objectively measured. For instance, defect density, customer satisfaction ratings, on-time delivery, or adherence to specifications.

Set Thresholds or Targets: Determine the desired targets or thresholds for each quality metric. These targets serve as benchmarks to gauge the success of the project in meeting the defined quality standards. Ensure that the targets are realistic, attainable, and aligned with stakeholder expectations.

Incorporate Quality Activities: Integrate quality activities into the project plan and schedule. Assign specific tasks and responsibilities related to quality assurance, quality control, and quality management. Consider activities such as inspections, reviews, testing, validation, and verification.

Establish Quality Assurance Processes: Develop processes and procedures to ensure that quality standards are followed consistently throughout the project. This includes activities such as defining quality checklists, conducting audits, performing peer reviews, and implementing quality assurance reviews.

Implement Quality Control Measures: Put in place measures to monitor and control the quality of project deliverables during their development. This involves activities such as conducting inspections, performing testing, tracking defects, and ensuring adherence to quality standards. Implement feedback loops to address and correct any identified quality issues.

Document and Communicate Quality Requirements: Clearly document the defined quality standards, metrics, and targets. Communicate these requirements to the project team, stakeholders, and suppliers Ensure that everyone involved understands the expected level of quality and their roles in achieving it.

Monitor and Evaluate Quality: Continuously monitor and evaluate the quality throughout the project's lifecycle. Measure the defined quality metrics and compare them against the established targets. Identify any deviations or trends that indicate potential quality issues. Take corrective action to fill in any gaps or shortcomings.

Review and Improve: Conduct regular reviews of the quality management processes and outcomes. Capture lessons learned and feedback from stakeholders. Use this information to identify areas for improvement, refine quality standards and metrics, and enhance the quality management approach for future projects.

By following these steps, you can establish clear quality standards and metrics that align with project objectives and stakeholder expectations. Regular monitoring and evaluation of quality ensure that project deliverables meet the defined criteria and contribute to overall project success.

6.3 Conducting Quality Reviews and Inspections

Conducting quality reviews and inspections is a critical part of ensuring that project deliverables meet the defined quality standards and requirements. These reviews and inspections help identify defects, errors, or deviations early in the project lifecycle, allowing for timely corrective actions. Here's a step-by-step approach to conducting quality reviews and inspections:

Define Review and Inspection Criteria: Determine the criteria against which the project deliverables will be evaluated during the reviews and inspections. These criteria should be aligned with the quality standards and metrics established for the project. Examples of criteria include completeness, accuracy, adherence to specifications, usability, and compliance with relevant regulations or standards.

Identify Review and Inspection Participants: Assemble a group of qualified individuals who will be responsible for conducting the quality reviews and inspections. These individuals can include subject matter experts, stakeholders, end-users, and quality assurance personnel. Ensure that the reviewers have the necessary expertise and knowledge to assess the specific deliverable being reviewed.

Establish Review and Inspection Processes: Define the processes and procedures that will be followed during the quality reviews and inspections. Determine the types of documents or deliverables that will undergo review, the schedule and frequency of the reviews, and the methods to be used (e.g., document review, walkthroughs, peer inspections, or code reviews).

Conduct Document Reviews: Review project documents, such as requirements specifications, design documents, test plans, and user manuals, to ensure they meet the defined quality criteria. Verify that the documents are accurate, complete, and well-organized. Identify any inconsistencies, errors, or omissions that need to be addressed.

Perform Walkthroughs or Inspections: Conduct walkthroughs or inspections of project artifacts, such as software code, architectural diagrams, or prototypes. This involves a structured review process where the reviewers examine the deliverable in detail, looking for design flaws, coding errors, or potential usability issues. Use checklists or predefined criteria to guide the reviewers during the inspection.

Identify Defects and Issues: During the quality reviews and inspections, document any identified defects, errors, or issues. Capture detailed information about each item, including its nature, location, severity, and potential impact on the project. Classify the defects based on their priority or severity to aid in subsequent corrective actions.

Conduct Peer Reviews: Engage in peer reviews, where team members review each other's work to identify defects or improvements. This can involve code reviews, design reviews, or documentation reviews. Encourage an open and collaborative environment where constructive feedback is provided to enhance the quality of the deliverables.

Provide Feedback and Recommendations: Share the findings of the quality reviews and inspections with the relevant stakeholders, including the project team, management, and the individuals responsible for the deliverables. Provide clear and specific feedback on the identified defects or issues. Make recommendations for corrective actions or improvements based on the review outcomes.

Implement Corrective Actions: Initiate corrective actions to address the identified defects and issues. Assign responsibilities for resolving the identified problems and track their progress. Ensure that the necessary adjustments, fixes, or rework are carried out promptly and effectively.

Verify and Validate Fixes: Once the corrective actions have been implemented, conduct a follow-up review or inspection to verify that the identified defects have been addressed adequately. Validate that the fixes are effective and have not introduced new issues. Provide feedback and guidance for further improvements, if necessary.

Document Lessons Learned: Capture lessons learned from the quality reviews and inspections. Document best practices, common issues, and recommendations for future projects. Use this knowledge to improve processes, tools, and the overall quality management approach for subsequent projects.

By following these steps, you can effectively conduct quality reviews and inspections, enabling early identification of defects and ensuring that project deliverables meet the defined quality standards. This promotes continuous improvement, reduces rework, and enhances the overall quality of the project outcomes.

6.4 Continuous Improvement and Lessons Learned

Continuous improvement and learning from past experiences are essential for project success and organizational growth. They enable you to identify areas for improvement, capitalize on lessons learned, and enhance future project performance. Here's how you can foster continuous improvement and effectively capture lessons learned:

Foster a Culture of Learning: Create an environment that encourages open communication, collaboration, and a willingness to learn and improve. Foster a culture where team members feel comfortable sharing their experiences, insights, and ideas for improvement.

Conduct Post-Project Reviews: After each project, conduct a comprehensive review to evaluate its overall performance, including achievements, challenges, and lessons learned. Involve the project team, stakeholders, and key individuals who were directly involved in the project. Assess the project against its objectives, scope, schedule, budget, and quality criteria.

Identify Successes and Challenges: Identify and document the successes and achievements of the project. Recognize and celebrate the positive outcomes, best practices, and lessons learned from successful project components. Similarly, identify the challenges, issues, and areas for improvement that were encountered during the project.

Capture Lessons Learned: Systematically capture lessons learned throughout the project lifecycle. This can include documenting successes, challenges, best practices, and improvement opportunities. Encourage project team members to share their insights and observations regarding project management processes, technical aspects, stakeholder management, or any other relevant areas.

Analyze Lessons Learned: Analyze the captured lessons learned to identify common themes, trends, and root causes behind successes and challenges. Look for recurring issues, patterns, or gaps that can inform improvements in future projects. Use this analysis to generate actionable recommendations and insights.

Document and Share Knowledge: Create a repository or knowledge management system to capture and organize lessons learned, best practices, and project-related knowledge. Document the lessons learned in a structured and accessible format. Make this knowledge readily available to the project team and other stakeholders involved in similar projects.

Implement Improvements: Develop action plans to implement the identified improvements based on the lessons learned. Assign responsibilities, set timelines, and track progress on implementing these improvements. Ensure that the changes are communicated effectively and integrated into project management processes, methodologies, and tools.

Encourage Continuous Feedback: Establish mechanisms for ongoing feedback and improvement throughout the project lifecycle. Encourage project team members, stakeholders, and customers to provide feedback on project performance, processes, and deliverables. Regularly solicit suggestions for improvement and address them in a timely manner.

Conduct Periodic Process Assessments: Periodically assess project management processes, methodologies, and tools. Evaluate their effectiveness, efficiency, and alignment with industry best practices. Identify areas for refinement or enhancement and implement necessary adjustments to optimize project management practices.

Promote Continuous Learning: Encourage ongoing professional development and learning opportunities for project team members. Provide training, workshops, or resources to enhance their skills and knowledge in project management disciplines. Support certifications and encourage participation in conferences or industry events.

Monitor and Evaluate Improvement Efforts: Continuously monitor and evaluate the effectiveness of the implemented improvements. Assess their impact on project performance, team dynamics, stakeholder satisfaction, and overall project outcomes. Adjust the improvement efforts as needed based on feedback and results.

Share and Apply Lessons Learned Organization-Wide: Share the lessons learned and improvements achieved across the organization. Foster cross-project learning and collaboration by disseminating knowledge and insights to other project teams. Incorporate the lessons learned into organizational project management methodologies and practices.

By embracing continuous improvement and actively capturing and applying lessons learned, you can enhance project performance, minimize risks, and drive ongoing organizational growth and success.

CHAPTER 7

STAKEHOLDER MANAGEMENT

7.1 Need for a stakeholder management

Stakeholder management is a critical aspect of project management that involves identifying, analyzing, and effectively engaging with individuals or groups who have a vested interest in or are impacted by the project. Stakeholders can include project sponsors, clients, team members, users, suppliers, regulators, and the broader community. Here are some key reasons why stakeholder management is crucial in project management:

Project Success: Stakeholder management significantly influences project success. Engaging stakeholders early on and understanding their needs, expectations, and concerns helps in setting clear project objectives and aligning them with stakeholder interests. By actively managing stakeholders throughout the project, project managers can enhance stakeholder satisfaction, secure necessary support, and increase the likelihood of project success.

Stakeholder Identification: Effective stakeholder management begins with identifying all relevant stakeholders. Each stakeholder brings a unique perspective, influence, or interest that can impact the project. By systematically identifying stakeholders, project managers can ensure that no important perspectives are overlooked and develop appropriate strategies to engage and communicate with them.

Communication and Collaboration: Stakeholder management is closely linked to effective communication and collaboration. Engaging stakeholders enables project managers to establish open channels of communication, foster collaboration, and build strong relationships. Regular and transparent communication with stakeholders ensures that they are informed about project progress, changes, and decisions, reducing uncertainty and increasing support.

Risk Management: Stakeholder management plays a critical role in identifying and managing project risks. By understanding stakeholders' concerns, expectations, and potential risks they may pose, project managers can proactively address these issues, mitigate risks, and avoid potential conflicts that could negatively impact project outcomes.

Resource Allocation: Stakeholders often play a vital role in providing resources, whether it be financial, personnel, or other forms of support. Effective stakeholder management helps in securing necessary resources by engaging stakeholders, demonstrating the value of the project, and building strong relationships based on trust and mutual understanding.

Change Management: Projects often involve change, and stakeholders are directly affected by these changes. By engaging stakeholders early on, project managers can anticipate potential resistance, identify change champions, and develop change management strategies to address concerns, minimize resistance, and facilitate smooth project implementation.

Reputation and Public Image: Stakeholder perception and satisfaction can significantly impact an organization's reputation and public image. Effective stakeholder management allows project managers to proactively address stakeholder concerns, manage expectations, and ensure that the project is aligned with stakeholders' values. By maintaining positive relationships and managing stakeholder perceptions, the project and the organization's overall reputation can be enhanced.

Legal and Ethical Considerations: Stakeholder management ensures that the project complies with legal and ethical standards. Engaging relevant stakeholders, particularly regulators and industry bodies, helps in understanding and adhering to legal requirements, standards, and guidelines, mitigating legal risks and ensuring ethical project practices.

Stakeholder management is essential in project management as it influences project success, enhances communication and collaboration, mitigates risks, secures resources, facilitates change management, protects reputation, and ensures compliance with legal and ethical standards. By effectively managing stakeholders, project managers can foster positive relationships, gain support, and navigate project challenges, ultimately leading to successful project outcomes.

7.2 Identifying and Prioritizing Stakeholders

Identifying and prioritizing stakeholders is a crucial step in project management to ensure effective communication, engagement, and management of stakeholders' interests and expectations. Here's how you can identify and prioritize stakeholders:

Identify Stakeholders: Start by identifying all individuals, groups, organizations, or entities that have an interest in or can be impacted by the project. This includes internal stakeholders such as project team members, management, and employees, as well as external stakeholders such as customers, suppliers, regulators, and the community. Use techniques like brainstorming, interviews, and stakeholder analysis to comprehensively identify stakeholders.

Categorize Stakeholders: Categorize the identified stakeholders based on their level of influence, power, and interest in the project. This can help prioritize and tailor engagement strategies for each stakeholder category. Common stakeholder categories include primary stakeholders (directly affected by the project), secondary stakeholders (indirectly affected), key stakeholders (with high influence or power), and low priority stakeholders (with low influence or interest).

Assess Stakeholder Interests and Expectations: Conduct a stakeholder analysis to understand the interests, expectations, and needs of each stakeholder. Consider their potential impact on the project and the level of support or resistance they may exhibit. Identify their goals, concerns, priorities, and desired project outcomes. This analysis helps in developing appropriate strategies to manage stakeholder engagement effectively.

Prioritize Stakeholders: Prioritize stakeholders based on their level of influence, power, and impact on the project, as well as their level of interest and support. High-priority stakeholders are those who have significant influence, high power, and strong interest in the project's success. They require focused attention and proactive engagement. Lower-priority stakeholders may require less intensive engagement efforts.

Engage Stakeholders: Develop a stakeholder engagement plan that outlines the specific strategies, activities, and communication channels to engage and manage each stakeholder group. Tailor the engagement approach based on the stakeholders' interests, expectations, and level of priority. Consider their preferred communication methods, frequency of engagement, and information needs.

Maintain Ongoing Communication: Establish and maintain open lines of communication with stakeholders throughout the project. Regularly communicate project updates, progress, milestones, and any changes that may impact stakeholders. Seek feedback, address concerns, and actively involve stakeholders in decision-making processes when appropriate.

Adapt and Adjust: Continuously monitor and reassess stakeholder priorities and dynamics throughout the project lifecycle. Stakeholders' interests, priorities, and influence may change over time. Be flexible and adaptable in adjusting the stakeholder engagement strategies and approaches based on evolving needs and circumstances.

Resolve Conflicts: Anticipate and address conflicts or disagreements among stakeholders promptly and constructively. Facilitate dialogue, negotiation, and consensus-building processes to resolve conflicts and reach mutually beneficial outcomes. Engage in active stakeholder management to minimize conflicts and foster collaboration.

Evaluate Stakeholder Engagement: Regularly assess the effectiveness of stakeholder engagement efforts. Evaluate the level of stakeholder satisfaction, the quality of communication, and the degree to which stakeholder interests are incorporated into project decisions. Use feedback and lessons learned to continuously improve stakeholder management practices.

Remember, stakeholder identification and prioritization is an iterative process. The stakeholder landscape may evolve, and new stakeholders may emerge as the project progresses. Stay vigilant and proactive in managing stakeholder engagement to ensure successful project outcomes and stakeholder satisfaction.

7.3 Managing Expectations and Communication

Managing expectations and communication is crucial for successful project management. It involves effectively setting, aligning, and managing stakeholder expectations while ensuring clear and timely communication throughout the project. Here are some steps to manage expectations and communication:

Identify Stakeholders: Identify all relevant stakeholders who have an interest in or can be affected by the project. This includes both internal and external stakeholders such as project team members, management, customers, suppliers, and regulatory bodies.

Understand Stakeholder Expectations: Engage with stakeholders to understand their expectations, needs, and desired outcomes from the project. Conduct stakeholder analysis to identify their goals, concerns, priorities, and potential areas of conflict.

Set Realistic Expectations: Based on the project objectives, scope, constraints, and stakeholder input, set realistic and achievable expectations. Ensure that stakeholders have a clear understanding of what can be delivered and any limitations that may exist.

Communicate Project Objectives: Clearly communicate the project objectives, including the desired outcomes and benefits. Explain how the project aligns with the strategic goals of the organization or stakeholders. Make sure everyone understands by using clear, succinct wording.

Develop a Communication Plan: Develop a communication plan that outlines the key messages, target audiences, communication channels, and frequency of communication. Tailor the plan to meet the needs and preferences of different stakeholders. Consider using a variety of communication methods such as meetings, emails, reports, and project management tools.

Establish Two-Way Communication: Foster open and transparent communication channels that allow stakeholders to provide feedback, ask questions, and express concerns. Encourage active listening and ensure that stakeholders feel heard and understood. Establish a culture of collaboration and shared responsibility.

Regularly Share Project Updates: Provide regular project updates to stakeholders, keeping them informed about project progress, milestones achieved, and any changes or challenges encountered. Clearly communicate any deviations from the original plan and explain the impact on the project objectives and timeline.

Manage Change Effectively: When changes to the project scope, schedule, or requirements occur, promptly communicate the reasons, implications, and proposed solutions to stakeholders. Involve them in the decision-making process and manage their expectations regarding the changes.

Address Concerns and Issues: Actively address stakeholder concerns and issues that arise during the project. Listen attentively, empathize with their perspectives, and work collaboratively to find appropriate resolutions. Update stakeholders on how the problem is being resolved.

Document Decisions and Agreements: Maintain clear records of project decisions, agreements, and changes. Document meeting minutes, action items, and any modifications to the project plan. Share these documents with relevant stakeholders to ensure alignment and avoid misunderstandings.

Monitor Stakeholder Satisfaction: Regularly assess stakeholder satisfaction levels by soliciting feedback through surveys, interviews, or other feedback mechanisms. Use the feedback to identify areas for improvement and make necessary adjustments to communication and project management approaches.

Adapt Communication Styles: Tailor your communication style and approach to suit the preferences and needs of different stakeholders. Consider factors such as their level of expertise, cultural background, communication preferences, and preferred level of detail. Adapt your language, tone, and messaging to ensure effective communication.

Celebrate Milestones and Successes: Recognize and celebrate project milestones and successes with stakeholders. Acknowledge their contributions and express gratitude for their support. Celebrating achievements fosters positive relationships and reinforces stakeholder engagement.

By managing expectations and maintaining effective communication, you can build trust, mitigate misunderstandings, and ensure that stakeholders remain engaged and supportive throughout the project. This enhances project success and stakeholder satisfaction.

7.4 Resolving Stakeholder Conflicts

Resolving stakeholder conflicts is essential for maintaining positive relationships and ensuring project success. Conflicts can arise due to differing interests, priorities, or perspectives among stakeholders. Here are some steps to effectively manage and resolve stakeholder conflicts:

Identify the Underlying Issues: Understand the root causes of the conflict by actively listening to the concerns and perspectives of the conflicting stakeholders. Identify the specific issues or points of disagreement and ensure a clear understanding of each stakeholder's interests, goals, and concerns.

Facilitate Open Communication: Create a safe and constructive environment for stakeholders to express their viewpoints and concerns. Encourage open and honest dialogue, ensuring that all parties have an opportunity to be heard and understood. Actively listen to each stakeholder's perspective without bias or judgment.

Seek Common Ground: Identify areas of common interest or shared goals among conflicting stakeholders. Focus on finding common ground and shared objectives that can serve as a basis for collaboration and resolution. Emphasize the collective benefit and seek win-win solutions that address the concerns of all parties.

Collaborative Problem-Solving: Engage conflicting stakeholders in a collaborative problem-solving process. Facilitate discussions to explore potential solutions and alternatives. Encourage stakeholders to generate ideas and proposals to address the conflict. Promote brainstorming, negotiation, and consensus-building techniques to find mutually acceptable resolutions.

Mediation or Facilitation: In situations where the conflict persists or becomes more complex, consider involving a neutral third party as a mediator or facilitator. A skilled mediator can help guide the discussion, manage emotions, and assist in finding common ground and mutually agreeable solutions.

Prioritize the Project's Best Interest: Keep the project's best interest at the forefront of conflict resolution efforts. Focus on the project's objectives, scope, schedule, and overall success. Encourage stakeholders to align their perspectives and actions with the project's goals and prioritize its success over individual or departmental interests.

Explore Compromises: In some cases, stakeholders may need to make compromises or trade-offs to reach a resolution. Encourage stakeholders to consider the bigger picture and explore options for compromise that still meet their essential needs and maintain the project's progress.

Document Agreements: Once a resolution is reached, document the agreements and decisions made by all parties involved. Ensure that there is a shared understanding of the resolution, including any changes to project plans, scope, or agreements. This documentation serves as a reference point and helps prevent future misunderstandings.

Monitor and Follow Up: After conflict resolution, monitor the situation and assess whether the agreed-upon solutions are being implemented effectively. Follow up with stakeholders to ensure ongoing satisfaction and address any concerns that may arise during the project's progress. Take proactive measures to prevent the conflict from reemerging.

Learn from the Conflict: Use the conflict as an opportunity for learning and improvement. Reflect on the causes of the conflict and identify preventive measures that can be incorporated into future projects. Capture lessons learned and share them with the project team and stakeholders to enhance future conflict resolution processes.

Remember, resolving stakeholder conflicts requires patience, empathy, and effective communication. By addressing conflicts promptly and finding mutually acceptable solutions, you can foster collaboration, maintain stakeholder satisfaction, and support the successful delivery of the project.

CHAPTER 8

PROJECT CLOSURE

Project closure is the final phase in project management that marks the formal conclusion of a project. It involves a series of activities aimed at wrapping up all project-related tasks, documenting lessons learned, and transitioning the project deliverables to the appropriate stakeholders. The project closure phase is crucial for evaluating the project's success, capturing valuable insights, and ensuring a smooth transition into post-project operations.

One of the primary activities during project closure is the completion of all outstanding tasks and finalizing project deliverables. This includes obtaining client acceptance, conducting final inspections, and ensuring that all project requirements and objectives have been met. Additionally, the project closure phase involves conducting a thorough review and analysis of the project's performance, including an assessment of the project's adherence to the schedule, budget, and quality standards. Lessons learned from the project are documented, capturing both successful practices and areas for improvement. This knowledge is invaluable for future projects, as it helps in refining project management methodologies and enhancing organizational capabilities.

Another critical aspect of project closure is the formal handover of the project's outputs to the appropriate stakeholders. This involves ensuring that all necessary documentation, such as user manuals, training materials, and maintenance guidelines, are provided to the end users or operational teams. Any outstanding contracts, agreements, or financial obligations are settled, and the project team is disbanded or transitioned into new roles within the organization.

Overall, project closure provides an opportunity to reflect on the project's accomplishments, capture lessons learned, and celebrate the successful completion of the project. It enables the organization to leverage the knowledge gained and improve future project outcomes. Properly closing a project ensures a smooth transition to post-project operations and sets the stage for future endeavors.

8.1 Evaluating Project Success and Lessons Learned

Evaluating project success and capturing lessons learned are essential for continuous improvement and enhancing future project performance. Here's a step-by-step approach to evaluating project success and effectively capturing lessons learned:

Define Success Criteria:

Clearly define the success criteria at the outset of the project. These criteria should be specific, measurable, attainable, relevant, and time-bound (SMART).

Example success criteria may include completing the project within the allocated budget, delivering all project deliverables on time, achieving a customer satisfaction rating of at least 90%, and meeting all quality standards defined for the project.

The success criteria should align with the project's objectives and be agreed upon by relevant stakeholders.

Measure Performance:

Regularly track and measure project performance against the defined success criteria and KPIs. This can involve collecting data on key project parameters such as cost, schedule, quality, and customer satisfaction.

Analyze the collected data to assess how the project is progressing and performing. Compare actual performance against the planned targets to identify any deviations or variances.

Use performance metrics to gauge the project's health and identify areas requiring improvement or corrective actions.

Regularly report performance updates to stakeholders to keep them informed about the project's progress.

Conduct Post-Project Evaluation:

Conduct a comprehensive evaluation of the project after its completion or at significant milestones. This evaluation assesses the project's overall success in meeting its objectives and delivering value to stakeholders.

Evaluate the project's performance against the defined success criteria and KPIs. Compare actual results against the planned targets to determine the level of achievement.

Assess the project's impact on the organization, stakeholders, and business outcomes. Consider factors such as financial benefits, customer satisfaction, stakeholder engagement, and lessons learned.

Analyze the reasons behind any deviations or variances and identify the root causes to inform future improvements.

Analyze Variances:

Analyze any variances or deviations from the planned targets. Evaluate the impact of these variances on the project's objectives, timeline, budget, and quality.

Identify the root causes of the variances, considering factors such as changes in requirements, unforeseen risks, resource constraints, or external factors.

Analyzing variances helps identify lessons learned and opportunities for process improvements in future projects.

It is essential to differentiate between controllable and uncontrollable variances to focus improvement efforts effectively.

Capture Lessons Learned:

Facilitate lessons learned sessions or workshops involving project team members and key stakeholders. Encourage open and honest discussions to capture insights, best practices, challenges, and recommendations.

Document lessons learned from the project in a structured format. Ensure that the documentation is clear, concise, and includes actionable recommendations.

Lessons learned may include identifying successful strategies, highlighting areas for improvement, documenting project management best practices, and sharing knowledge gained during the project.

It is crucial to capture both positive and negative lessons to foster continuous improvement.

Document Lessons Learned:

Document the lessons learned in a structured format, such as a lessons learned report or knowledge repository. Ensure that the documentation captures the project context, specific lessons, and their impact on project outcomes.

Include detailed information about the identified lessons, their causes, and the recommended actions for improvement.

Clearly articulate the insights gained, best practices identified, and recommendations for future projects.

Ensure that the lessons learned documentation is easily accessible and shareable within the organization.

Share Lessons Learned:

Share the documented lessons learned with the project team, stakeholders, and other relevant individuals or teams within the organization.

Disseminate the knowledge gained from the project to promote learning and improvement across the organization.

Use various communication channels such as reports, presentations, knowledge management systems, or internal newsletters to share the lessons learned effectively.

Encourage feedback and discussion around the lessons learned to foster a culture of continuous learning and improvement.

Implement Improvements:

Based on the lessons learned, identify specific actions and improvements thatcan be implemented in future projects or project management processes.

Develop action plans that outline the steps, resources, and timelines required to implement the identified improvements.

Assign responsibilities to individuals or teams for implementing the improvement actions.

Set clear and measurable objectives for each improvement action.

Regularly review and track the progress of the improvement initiatives to ensure their effective implementation.

Continuously Improve:

Integrate the lessons learned and improvement actions into project management practices and methodologies.

Continuously refine and enhance project management processes based on the identified areas for improvement.

Encourage a culture of continuous learning and improvement within the organization by promoting knowledge sharing, training opportunities, and the adoption of best practices.

Regularly assess the effectiveness of the implemented improvements and make adjustments as needed to optimize project performance and outcomes.

Monitor and Review:

Continuously monitor project performance and evaluate the effectiveness of the implemented improvements.

Assess the impact of the improvements on future projects, stakeholder satisfaction, and project outcomes.

Regularly review and analyze feedback from stakeholders to identify additional areas for improvement.

Use a feedback loop to continuously learn from project experiences and adjust project management practices accordingly.

Establish a system to capture and share ongoing lessons learned to facilitate organizational learning and improvement.

8.2 Conducting Project Reviews and Documentation

Conducting project reviews and documentation is an essential part of project management to assess project performance, identify areas for improvement, and document project information for future reference. Here's an expanded explanation of conducting project reviews and documentation:

Conduct Regular Project Reviews:

Schedule and conduct regular project reviews throughout the project lifecycle. These reviews can occur at significant milestones, after project phases, or at predefined intervals.

Involve key stakeholders, project team members, and subject matter experts in the review process.

Evaluate the project's progress, adherence to the plan, and overall performance against the defined success criteria and objectives.

Assess the project's scope, schedule, budget, quality, risks, and stakeholder satisfaction.

Review the effectiveness of project management processes and methodologies.

Evaluate Project Performance:

Evaluating project performance is a crucial aspect of project management as it provides valuable insights into the project's progress, achievements, and areas for improvement. Effective evaluation helps project managers and stakeholders understand whether the project is meeting its objectives, staying on track, and delivering the expected value. Here are key steps and considerations for evaluating project performance:

Establish Clear Objectives and Success Criteria: Before evaluating project performance, it's important to establish clear project objectives and success criteria. They ought to be SMART objectives—specific, measurable, achievable, relevant, and time-bound. Well-defined objectives and criteria serve as benchmarks for evaluating progress and determining project success.

Define Key Performance Indicators (KPIs): Key Performance Indicators are quantifiable metrics that measure various aspects of project performance. KPIs should align with project objectives and provide meaningful insights. Examples of KPIs include project schedule adherence, budget variance, customer satisfaction ratings, quality metrics, and team performance indicators.

Monitor Progress Regularly: Regular monitoring is essential to evaluate project performance. Project managers should track and review project activities, milestones, deliverables, and resource utilization against the defined objectives and KPIs. This helps identify any deviations, bottlenecks, or risks that may impact project success.

Conduct Periodic Reviews: Periodic reviews provide opportunities to assess project performance holistically. These reviews can be conducted at key project milestones, phase completions, or at regular intervals. Project managers should analyze the project's progress, budget, schedule, quality, risks, and stakeholder feedback during these reviews. This facilitates identifying areas of improvement, making necessary adjustments, and ensuring alignment with project goals.

Use Earned Value Management (EVM): EVM is a powerful technique to evaluate project performance by integrating cost, schedule, and scope measurements. It helps project managers assess whether the project is delivering value in line with the planned budget and schedule. EVM calculates metrics such as Earned Value (EV), Actual Cost (AC), and Planned Value (PV), enabling comparisons and forecasting of project performance.

Engage Stakeholders: Engaging stakeholders in the evaluation process provides valuable perspectives and feedback. Stakeholders can offer insights on project performance, identify areas of concern, and suggest improvements. Regular communication with stakeholders helps project managers understand their expectations, address issues promptly, and maintain stakeholder satisfaction.

Conduct Post-Project Reviews: After project completion, conducting post-project reviews, also known as lessons learned sessions, is essential. This involves analyzing the project's overall performance, successes, challenges, and the effectiveness of project management practices. Post-project reviews provide valuable insights for future projects, facilitating continuous improvement and knowledge transfer within the organization.

Document and Report Findings: It is important to document the findings and results of the project performance evaluation. Clear and concise reports should be prepared, highlighting the project's achievements, areas for improvement, and recommendations for future projects. These reports serve as valuable references for project stakeholders and contribute to organizational learning.

Implement Corrective Actions: Evaluation is meaningless without taking corrective actions based on the findings. Project managers should analyze the evaluation results and identify necessary corrective actions to address performance gaps, mitigate risks, and enhance project outcomes. Implementing these actions in a timely manner ensures continuous project improvement.

Embrace Continuous Improvement: Evaluation should be an ongoing process throughout the project lifecycle. By embracing a culture of continuous improvement, project managers can proactively evaluate performance, learn from experiences, and apply lessons learned to future projects. Continuous improvement ensures that project management practices evolve and mature, leading to better outcomes and organizational success.

Evaluating project performance is essential to assess progress, measure achievements, and identify areas for improvement. By establishing clear objectives, defining KPIs, monitoring progress, engaging stakeholders, and conducting thorough evaluations, project managers can optimize project outcomes, enhance project management practices, and drive organizational success..

Identify Lessons Learned:

Lessons learned in project management are valuable insights gained from past project experiences. They represent knowledge and best practices that can be applied to future projects to improve project performance, avoid mistakes, and enhance overall project management effectiveness.

Effective Communication is Key: Clear and consistent communication among project stakeholders is crucial for project success. Lessons learned emphasize the importance of establishing open channels of communication, ensuring stakeholders are well-informed, and addressing conflicts or misunderstandings promptly.

Comprehensive Planning is Essential: Adequate project planning is a vital lesson learned. It emphasizes the need for thorough upfront planning, including defining project scope, setting realistic goals, creating a detailed project schedule, and developing a comprehensive project management plan. Proper planning minimizes risks, facilitates resource allocation, and increases the chances of achieving project objectives.

Stakeholder Engagement is Critical: Engaging stakeholders throughout the project lifecycle is a key lesson learned. This includes identifying stakeholders, understanding their needs and expectations, involving them in decision-making processes, and addressing their concerns. Effective stakeholder engagement helps build support, manage expectations, and ensure project success.

Risk Management is a Necessity: Proactive risk management is highlighted as a critical lesson learned. Projects are inherently uncertain, and identifying, assessing, and mitigating risks is essential. Lessons learned emphasize the importance of conducting thorough risk assessments, developing contingency plans, and continuously monitoring and addressing risks throughout the project.

Resource Management Requires Attention: Efficient resource management is a lesson learned to ensure optimal utilization of resources. This includes identifying resource requirements, allocating resources effectively, and monitoring resource availability and utilization. Lessons learned also stress the importance of addressing resource constraints and proactively managing dependencies.

Change Management is Vital: Change management plays a crucial role in project success. Lessons learned emphasize the need for a structured approach to managing change, including clearly communicating changes, addressing resistance, and providing adequate training and support to affected stakeholders.

Documentation and Knowledge Management: Proper documentation of project activities, decisions, and lessons learned is crucial. Lessons learned stress the importance of maintaining accurate records, capturing project knowledge, and creating a repository for future reference. This ensures that valuable insights and best practices are preserved and can be effectively shared across projects.

Quality Assurance and Control: Lessons learned emphasize the significance of quality assurance and control processes. This includes establishing quality standards, conducting regular inspections, performing testing and validation, and ensuring that deliverables meet the required quality criteria.

Team Collaboration and Leadership: Lessons learned highlight the importance of effective team collaboration and leadership. Encouraging teamwork, fostering a positive work environment, providing clear direction and support, and empowering team members to take ownership of their tasks contribute to project success.

Continuous Improvement: Continuous improvement is a recurring lesson learned in project management. Projects offer opportunities for learning and growth. Lessons learned stress the importance of conducting post-project reviews, capturing lessons and insights, and applying them to future projects to enhance project management practices continually.

By embracing lessons learned in project management, organizations can foster a culture of continuous improvement, avoid common pitfalls, and increase the likelihood of project success. These lessons provide valuable guidance for project managers and teams, enabling them to deliver projects more effectively and efficiently.

Document Project Information:

Documenting project information is an essential practice in project management. It involves capturing and organizing key project details, decisions, processes, and outcomes to ensure that relevant information is readily available for reference, communication, and future use. Here are important aspects of project information that should be documented:

Project Charter: The project charter serves as a foundational document that outlines the project's objectives, scope, stakeholders, high-level requirements, and initial constraints. It provides a clear understanding of the project's purpose and direction.

Project Management Plan: The project management plan is a comprehensive document that outlines the project's approach, methodologies, roles and responsibilities, communication plan, risk management strategies, quality management procedures, and other essential project management components. It serves as a roadmap for project execution and control.

Project Scope Statement: The project scope statement defines the project's boundaries, deliverables, and objectives. It outlines what is included and excluded from the project, ensuring a shared understanding among stakeholders.

Work Breakdown Structure (WBS): The WBS breaks down the project's scope into smaller, manageable work packages, tasks, or activities. It provides a hierarchical structure that facilitates planning, resource allocation, and tracking progress.

Project Schedule: The project schedule documents the planned start and end dates of project activities, milestones, and dependencies. It provides a timeline for project execution, enabling effective resource management, task sequencing, and progress monitoring.

Risk Register: The risk register captures identified risks, their probability and impact assessments, mitigation or response strategies, and assigned responsibilities. It serves as a central repository for managing project risks throughout the project lifecycle.

Issue Log: The issue log records any problems, challenges, or obstacles encountered during project execution. It includes details such as the issue description, impact, priority, assigned owner, and status. The issue log helps in tracking and resolving project issues promptly.

Change Control Documentation: Any changes to the project's scope, schedule, or resources should be documented in change control documentation. This includes change requests, change impact assessments, approval records, and updated project documentation reflecting the approved changes.

Meeting Minutes: Documenting meeting minutes captures key discussions, decisions, and action items from project meetings. It ensures that participants have a clear understanding of what was discussed, agreed upon, and assigned for follow-up.

Lessons Learned: Documenting lessons learned throughout the project captures valuable insights, best practices, and areas for improvement. It provides a repository of knowledge that can be utilized for future projects to avoid mistakes, enhance project performance, and promote continuous learning.

Project Reports: Regular project reports, such as status updates, progress reports, and milestone summaries, document the project's progress, achievements, challenges, and variances from the plan. These reports communicate project status to stakeholders and facilitate informed decision-making.

Documentation of Deliverables: Documenting project deliverables ensures that the final products, services, or outcomes of the project are captured accurately. It includes specifications, acceptance criteria, user manuals, and any other relevant documentation related to the project deliverables.

Effective project information documentation enhances project transparency, communication, and knowledge transfer. It provides a historical record of the project and facilitates seamless project management throughout its lifecycle. Additionally, proper documentation serves as a valuable resource for future reference, audits, and organizational learning.

Create Project Review Reports:

A project review report is a comprehensive document that assesses the overall performance, outcomes, and lessons learned from a completed project. It provides a structured analysis of the project's achievements, challenges, and recommendations for improvement. Here are key components typically included in a project review report in project management:

Executive Summary: This section provides a concise overview of the project review report, summarizing the project's objectives, outcomes, and key findings. It highlights the main recommendations and conclusions for management and stakeholders.

Introduction: The introduction sets the context for the project review report, providing background information about the project, its purpose, and the scope of the review. It outlines the objectives of the review and the methodology used.

Project Overview: This section provides an overview of the project, including the project's background, goals, scope, stakeholders, and key deliverables. It summarizes the project's timeline, budget, and resources allocated.

Evaluation of Project Performance: This section evaluates the project's performance against predefined metrics, goals, and key performance indicators (KPIs). It assesses the project's success in achieving its objectives, meeting deliverables, adhering to schedule and budget, and delivering the expected value.

Analysis of Achievements and Challenges: This section analyzes the project's achievements and challenges, highlighting notable successes and areas where the project faced difficulties or encountered obstacles. It explores factors that contributed to success or impeded progress and provides insights into how these factors can be replicated or mitigated in future projects.

Lessons Learned: This section captures lessons learned throughout the project lifecycle. It highlights both positive and negative experiences, identifies best practices, and suggests improvements for future projects. Lessons learned may cover areas such as project planning, stakeholder management, risk management, communication, resource allocation, and team collaboration.

Recommendations: Based on the project review findings and lessons learned, this section provides actionable recommendations for improving future project management practices. Recommendations may include specific actions to address identified challenges, optimize project processes, enhance stakeholder engagement, or implement changes to avoid similar issues in future projects.

Conclusion: The conclusion summarizes the key findings of the project review report, reiterating the project's achievements and challenges. It reinforces the significance of the lessons learned and recommendations provided.

Appendices: Appendices may include supporting documents, charts, graphs, or detailed data related to the project review. This can include project documents, risk registers, meeting minutes, and any other relevant information that adds value and context to the report.

The project review report serves as a valuable reference for project stakeholders, providing insights into project performance, identifying areas for improvement, and informing future project management decisions. It facilitates organizational learning, helps refine project management practices, and contributes to continuous improvement within the organization.

Share and Communicate Findings:

Sharing and effectively communicating findings in project management is crucial to ensure that stakeholders are informed, decisions are well-informed, and knowledge is disseminated for organizational learning. Here are some key considerations for sharing and communicating findings in project management:

Determine the Target Audience: Identify the stakeholders who need to be informed of the findings. This can include project sponsors, executives, team members, clients, and other relevant parties. Understanding their needs, expectations, and level of detail required will help tailor the communication appropriately.

Choose the Right Communication Channels: Select appropriate communication channels based on the nature of the findings and the preferences of the stakeholders. This can include face-to-face meetings, presentations, written reports, emails, project management software, or a combination of multiple channels. Consider using visual aids, charts, or diagrams to enhance understanding and engagement.

Craft a Clear and Concise Message: Condense the findings into a clear and concise message that conveys the key insights, outcomes, and recommendations. Avoid technical jargon or overly complex language and focus on presenting the information in a manner that is easily understood by the target audience.

Provide Sufficient Context: When sharing findings, provide the necessary context to help stakeholders understand the background, scope, and significance of the findings. Explain the methodology used, any limitations or assumptions made, and the implications of the findings on the project or organization.

Highlight Key Findings: Emphasize the most critical and impactful findings to grab the attention of stakeholders. Clearly articulate the successes, challenges, lessons learned, and any recommendations derived from the findings. Use data, examples, and real-life scenarios to illustrate and support the findings.

Engage in Two-Way Communication: Encourage interactive communication by allowing stakeholders to ask questions, provide feedback, and share their perspectives. Create a collaborative environment that fosters open dialogue and encourages stakeholders to contribute their insights and experiences related to the findings.

Tailor the Message to Different Stakeholders: Adapt the communication style and level of detail to suit the specific needs of different stakeholders. Executives may require a high-level summary, while project team members may benefit from more granular details. Customize the message to resonate with each stakeholder group and address their specific interests and concerns.

Follow-Up and Address Concerns: Be responsive to stakeholder queries, concerns, or feedback that may arise after sharing the findings. Follow up with additional information, clarification, or action plans as needed. Actively address any unresolved issues or uncertainties to ensure stakeholders feel heard and their concerns are adequately addressed.

Document and Archive the Findings: Document the findings, communication materials, and any additional discussions or decisions related to the findings. This helps maintain a record of the information shared and provides a reference for future use. Archiving the findings also contributes to organizational knowledge management.

Leverage Multiple Opportunities for Communication: Take advantage of various project milestones, meetings, status updates, and dedicated communication sessions to share the findings. Regularly update stakeholders on progress, changes, and actions taken based on the findings to ensure ongoing engagement and transparency.

By effectively sharing and communicating findings in project management, stakeholders are kept informed, decision-making is informed by reliable information, and lessons learned are disseminated throughout the organization. This fosters collaboration, enhances project outcomes, and contributes to continuous improvement in project management practices.

Update Project Documentation:

Update project documentation based on the findings and recommendations from project reviews.

Incorporate any changes, decisions, or modifications made during the project into the relevant project artifacts.

Ensure that project documentation accurately reflects the project's final state and outcomes.

Maintain an organized and up-to-date project repository for easy access and reference.

Use Project Documentation for Future Projects:

Utilize the project documentation as a valuable reference for future projects.

Draw insights from previous project experiences, best practices, and lessons learned.

Use the documented information to inform project planning, risk management, decision-making, and process improvement in future endeavors.

Share relevant project documentation with project teams or stakeholders involved in similar projects to benefit from past experiences.

By conducting project reviews and effectively documenting project information, you create a foundation for continuous improvement, knowledge sharing, and enhanced project management practices.

8.3 Celebrating Achievements and Recognizing Contributions

Celebrating achievements and recognizing contributions is an important aspect of project management that boosts morale, motivates the project team, and fosters a positive project culture. Here's an expanded explanation on how to celebrate achievements and recognize contributions:

Define Milestones and Success Criteria:

Establish clear milestones and success criteria at the beginning of the project. These milestones can be major project deliverables, key project phases, or significant achievements.

Define success criteria that align with the project's objectives and stakeholder expectations. This ensures that there are specific goals to celebrate and recognize.

Regularly Acknowledge Progress:

Acknowledge and celebrate progress as the project advances. Recognize small victories, milestones reached, and successful completion of project phases.

Communicate the progress to the project team, stakeholders, and relevant parties. Emphasize the positive outcomes achieved, such as meeting or exceeding targets, overcoming challenges, or delivering exceptional results.

Provide Timely and Specific Recognition:

Recognize individual and team contributions promptly and specifically. Highlight the unique efforts, skills, or achievements of team members.

Acknowledge both tangible and intangible contributions, such as technical expertise, collaboration, leadership, problem-solving, or going above and beyond expectations.

Personalize recognition to make it meaningful and impactful for the individuals involved.

Publicly Celebrate Achievements:

Publicly celebrate project achievements through various channels. This can include team meetings, newsletters, emails, announcements, or social media platforms.

Recognize achievements in a way that is visible and accessible to the wider organization or stakeholder community. This helps create a positive project reputation and increases visibility for the project team's efforts.

Organize Celebratory Events:

Organize events or gatherings to celebrate major milestones or project successes. These can be formal or informal, depending on the project and organizational culture.

Consider holding team lunches, award ceremonies, recognition ceremonies, or social events where team members can come together and celebrate collectively.

Use these events as opportunities to express appreciation, share success stories, and allow team members to reflect on their accomplishments.

Provide Rewards and Incentives:

Consider providing rewards or incentives to individuals or teams who have made significant contributions to the project's success. This can include bonuses, gift cards, certificates of achievement, or other tangible rewards.

Ensure that rewards are fair, transparent, and aligned with organizational policies and practices.

Acknowledge that recognition and rewards go beyond monetary value and can also include professional development opportunities, career advancement, or increased visibility within the organization.

Foster a Culture of Recognition:

Create a culture of recognition within the project team and the broader organization. Encourage your team to value and acknowledge each other's contributions.

Promote peer-to-peer recognition and create channels for team members to express gratitude and acknowledge each other's efforts.

Lead by example and consistently recognize and appreciate the work of team members, stakeholders, and other contributors.

Document and Share Success Stories:

Write down project success tales and lessons learned. Capture the challenges faced, innovative solutions implemented, and the impact of the project's achievements.

Share these success stories within the organization, using various communication channels such as newsletters, intranets, or presentations. This helps inspire others and demonstrates the project team's capabilities and accomplishments.

Learn from Celebrations and Recognitions:

Use celebrations and recognitions as an opportunity for learning and improvement. Encourage team members to reflect on the factors that contributed to the success and identify best practices to replicate in future projects.

Gather feedback from team members on the impact of celebrations and recognitions. Use this feedback to continually refine and enhance the recognition processes.

By celebrating achievements and recognizing contributions, project managers foster a positive project environment, inspire team members, and create a culture of appreciation and motivation. This, in turn, leads to increased morale, productivity, and overall project success.

CHAPTER 9

AGILE PROJECT MANAGEMENT

9.1 Introduction to Agile Methodologies

Agile methodologies are a set of approaches and principles that emphasize flexibility, collaboration, iterative development, and continuous improvement in software development and project management. Unlike traditional waterfall methods, which follow a linear and sequential approach, Agile methodologies embrace change, adaptability, and customer collaboration throughout the project lifecycle. Here's an introduction to Agile methodologies:

Agile Manifesto:

The Agile Manifesto, created by a group of software development practitioners, outlines the core values and principles of Agile methodologies.

It prioritizes individuals and interactions over processes and tools, working software over comprehensive documentation, customer collaboration over contract negotiation, and responding to change over following a plan.

Iterative and Incremental Development:

Agile methodologies promote iterative and incremental development, breaking down the project into smaller work cycles called iterations or sprints.

Each iteration delivers a functional increment of the project, allowing for continuous feedback and adjustment based on evolving requirements and stakeholder input.

Cross-functional Teams:

Agile emphasizes the importance of cross-functional teams that include members with different expertise and skills necessary for project success.

These teams are self-organizing and collaborate closely throughout the project, promoting effective communication, shared responsibility, and collective decision-making.

Scrum Framework:

One of the most popular Agile frameworks is Scrum. It divides the project into time-boxed iterations called sprints, typically lasting 1-4 weeks.

Scrum employs specific roles (such as Scrum Master, Product Owner, and Development Team), artifacts (such as Product Backlog and Sprint Backlog), and ceremonies (such as Daily Stand-ups, Sprint Planning, Sprint Review, and Retrospective) to structure and guide the project.

Kanban Method:

Kanban is another Agile methodology that visualizes work on a Kanban board, using columns and cards to represent tasks and their progress.

It focuses on limiting work in progress (WIP) to optimize workflow and promote continuous delivery. Kanban provides real-time visibility into the project's status and helps identify bottlenecks.

Lean Principles:

Agile methodologies draw inspiration from Lean principles, which aim to eliminate waste, improve efficiency, and maximize customer value.

Lean encourages continuous improvement, just-in-time delivery, and empowering teams to make decisions that improve the flow of work.

Adaptive Planning:

Agile methodologies emphasize adaptive planning, where plans and priorities are continuously reviewed and adjusted based on feedback, changing requirements, and emerging risks.

The project scope and priorities can be reevaluated at the end of each iteration to ensure alignment with the customer's needs and business goals.

Continuous Improvement:

Agile promotes a culture of continuous improvement, enabling teams to reflect on their processes and outcomes and identify opportunities for enhancement.

Through retrospectives, teams review their performance, celebrate successes, address challenges, and implement actionable improvements in subsequent iterations.

Customer Collaboration:

Agile methodologies prioritize active involvement and collaboration with customers or product owners throughout the project.

Regular feedback, demo sessions, and close interaction allow for evolving requirements, ensuring that the delivered product meets the customer's needs.

Embracing Change:

Agile methodologies welcome change as a natural part of the project. They are designed to be flexible and adaptable, enabling teams to respond to new insights, evolving market conditions, and shifting priorities.

Agile methodologies offer a flexible and customer-centric approach to project management, enabling teams to deliver high-quality products, respond to change, and continuously improve their processes. By embracing Agile principles, teams can enhance collaboration, increase productivity, and deliver value to stakeholders more effectively.

Agile planning and execution are key aspects of Agile methodologies, allowing teams to deliver projects iteratively and incrementally while adapting to changing requirements and feedback. Here's an overview of Agile planning and execution:

User Stories and Product Backlog:

Agile planning starts with capturing user requirements and prioritizing them as user stories. User stories describe the functionality or value that the end-user or customer expects from the product.

The user stories are organized into a product backlog, which is a prioritized list of all desired features, enhancements, and fixes for the product.

Sprint Planning:

In Agile, work is organized into time-boxed iterations called sprints. Sprint planning is a collaborative process where the development team selects a set of user stories from the product backlog to be completed during the upcoming sprint.

During sprint planning, the team breaks down the selected user stories into smaller tasks, estimates their effort, and determines how much work can be accomplished in the sprint.

Daily Stand-ups:

Daily stand-ups, also known as daily scrums, are short meetings held by the development team every day during a sprint. Team members provide updates on their progress since the last meeting, discuss any obstacles or challenges they are facing, and synchronize their activities.

The focus is on coordination, identifying and resolving impediments, and ensuring that everyone is aligned towards achieving the sprint goal.

Iterative Development:

Agile methodologies emphasize iterative development, where work is completed in short cycles or iterations.

Each iteration typically lasts from one to four weeks, during which the development team focuses on completing the selected user stories and delivering a potentially shippable product increment.

The product increment is a working version of the product with added features or functionality.

Continuous Integration and Testing:

Agile promotes continuous integration and testing practices to ensure that the product increment is integrated and tested frequently.

Developers regularly integrate their code changes into a shared repository, allowing for early detection and resolution of integration issues.

Automated testing is used to verify that the product meets the acceptance criteria defined for each user story.

Product Owner Involvement:

Throughout the Agile planning and execution process, the product owner plays a crucial role. The product owner represents the customer or end-user and is responsible for prioritizing the product backlog, clarifying requirements, and providing feedback.

The product owner collaborates closely with the development team, attends sprint planning, provides guidance during development, and reviews the completed work at the end of each sprint.

Sprint Review:

At the end of each sprint, a sprint review meeting is conducted to showcase the completed work to stakeholders, including the product owner and other relevant parties.

The development team demonstrates the product increment, explains the functionality that has been implemented, and gathers feedback.

The sprint review helps validate the work done, gather insights for future iterations, and ensure alignment with stakeholder expectations.

Retrospective:

After the sprint review, the team holds a retrospective meeting to reflect on the sprint's process, collaboration, and outcomes.

The retrospective focuses on identifying what worked well, what could be improved, and actionable steps for enhancing the team's effectiveness in future sprints.

The insights and lessons learned from the retrospective feed into the next sprint planning and contribute to continuous improvement.

Adaptation and Adjustments:

Agile planning and execution allow for flexibility and adaptation. As feedback is received and requirements evolve, adjustments can be made to the product backlog, sprint scope, and priorities.

Agile teams embrace change, leveraging frequent feedback and customer collaboration to adapt their plans and deliver maximum value.

Continuous Delivery:

Agile methodologies emphasize the concept of continuous delivery, where there is a focus on delivering valuable increments of the product at the end of each sprint.

By continuously delivering working and tested increments, Agile teams ensure that stakeholders receive tangible value throughout the project rather than waiting until the project's end.

Agile planning and execution promote flexibility, collaboration, and adaptability, allowing teams to deliver high-quality products that meet customer expectations. Through iterative development, continuous feedback, and regular reflection, Agile teams continuously improve their processes, enhance customer satisfaction, and deliver successful projects.

9.3 Adapting Agile Principles to Traditional Project Management

Adapting Agile principles to traditional project management involves incorporating Agile concepts and practices into the existing project management framework. By doing so, organizations can benefit from the flexibility, collaboration, and iterative approach of Agile methodologies while still adhering to traditional project management processes. Here are some ways to adapt Agile principles to traditional project management:

Embrace Iterative Planning:

Adopt an iterative planning approach by breaking down the project into phases or iterations.

Instead of creating a detailed project plan upfront, focus on planning one iteration at a time, allowing for adjustments and refinements as the project progresses.

Continuously assess and update the project plan, incorporating lessons learned and feedback from each iteration.

Prioritize and Deliver Incrementally:

Identify the most critical project requirements or deliverables and prioritize them based on business value or customer needs.

Plan and deliver these prioritized items incrementally, providing value to stakeholders early in the project.

Incorporate feedback from stakeholders to guide subsequent iterations and adjust priorities accordingly.

Foster Collaboration and Communication:

Promote collaboration and open communication among project team members, stakeholders, and other relevant parties.

Encourage cross-functional teams to work together, share information, and collaborate on project tasks and decisions.

Establish regular communication channels such as team meetings, status updates, and collaborative tools to facilitate real-time information sharing.

Embrace Change Management:

Recognize that change is inevitable and incorporate change management practices into the project management approach.

Maintain flexibility in the project plan to accommodate changing requirements or stakeholder needs.

Implement change control processes to evaluate and assess the impact of requested changes, ensuring they align with project objectives.

Adopt Continuous Improvement:

Encourage a culture of continuous improvement by regularly reflecting on project performance and seeking opportunities for enhancement.

Conduct project retrospectives to capture lessons learned and identify areas for improvement.

Implement improvements in subsequent iterations or future projects based on the insights gained from retrospectives.

Empower Self-Organizing Teams:

Promote self-organizing teams that have the autonomy to make decisions and collaborate on project tasks.

Encourage team members to take ownership of their work, share responsibilities, and contribute their expertise to achieve project goals.

Empower teams to identify and resolve issues, leveraging their collective knowledge and skills.

Continuously Monitor and Adapt:

Regularly monitor project progress, milestones, and performance metrics to track project health.

Incorporate feedback from stakeholders, team members, and project metrics to make data-driven decisions and adjust project plans as necessary.

Emphasize continuous monitoring and adaptation throughout the project lifecycle to ensure alignment with changing project conditions.

Focus on Value Delivery:

Align project activities and decisions with the delivery of value to stakeholders.

Continuously assess and prioritize project features, deliverables, or milestones based on their contribution to overall project value.

Regularly review and validate the delivered value with stakeholders to ensure alignment with their expectations.

By adapting Agile principles to traditional project management, organizations can introduce greater flexibility, collaboration, and adaptability into their project execution. This approach allows for iterative delivery, continuous improvement, and enhanced stakeholder satisfaction, leading to more successful project outcomes.

CHAPTER 10

ADVANCED PROJECT MANAGEMENT TECHNIQUES

Advanced project management techniques are specialized approaches and methodologies that go beyond the traditional project management practices. These techniques are designed to address complex projects, unique challenges, and specific industry requirements. Here are some advanced project management techniques:

Critical Chain Method (CCM):

The Critical Chain Method focuses on resource optimization and managing project schedule uncertainty.

It involves identifying the critical chain of tasks that determines the project's overall duration and strategically managing project resources to minimize delays.

CCM takes into account resource dependencies, buffers, and resource leveling techniques to ensure efficient project execution.

Earned Value Management (EVM):

Earned Value Management is a performance measurement technique that integrates scope, schedule, and cost to assess project performance.

It involves comparing the planned value, earned value, and actual cost of work performed to track project progress, identify variances, and forecast future performance.

EVM provides metrics such as Cost Performance Index (CPI) and Schedule Performance Index (SPI) to evaluate project efficiency and effectiveness.

Agile and Hybrid Approaches:

Agile methodologies, such as Scrum and Kanban, offer iterative and flexible project management techniques that adapt to changing requirements and foster collaboration.

Hybrid approaches combine elements of Agile and traditional project management, allowing organizations to tailor their project management practices to specific project needs.

Adopting Agile and hybrid approaches requires a shift in mindset, embracing adaptive planning, cross-functional teams, and iterative delivery.

Risk Management Techniques:

Advanced risk management techniques focus on proactive identification, assessment, and mitigation of project risks.

Techniques such as Monte Carlo simulation, decision tree analysis, and sensitivity analysis provide quantitative insights into the potential impact of risks on project outcomes.

Risk response strategies, such as risk avoidance, mitigation, transfer, or acceptance, are employed to minimize the negative impact of risks on project objectives.

Lean Project Management:

Lean project management applies Lean principles, originally derived from Lean manufacturing, to project management.

It aims to eliminate waste, optimize processes, and enhance value delivery.

Techniques such as value stream mapping, process flow analysis, and continuous improvement are used to streamline project workflows, reduce waste, and enhance project efficiency.

Virtual and Distributed Project Management:

With the rise of remote work and global project teams, virtual and distributed project management techniques have become increasingly important.

These techniques focus on effective communication, collaboration, and coordination across geographically dispersed teams.

Tools such as virtual meeting platforms, cloud-based project management software, and collaboration tools facilitate seamless information sharing and real-time collaboration.

Project Portfolio Management (PPM):

Project Portfolio Management is a strategic approach that involves selecting, prioritizing, and managing a portfolio of projects to align with organizational objectives.

PPM techniques include portfolio analysis, resource allocation, risk assessment, and benefits realization to ensure optimal resource utilization and maximize overall project portfolio value.

Change Management:

Advanced change management techniques address the people side of project implementation, ensuring successful adoption of project deliverables and managing resistance to change.

Techniques such as stakeholder analysis, communication planning, training, and organizational change readiness assessments help facilitate smooth transitions and minimize the negative impact of change on project outcomes.

Advanced Project Reporting and Analytics:

Advanced project reporting techniques leverage data analytics, visualization tools, and dashboards to provide real-time project insights and facilitate data-driven decision-making.

Techniques such as project performance dashboards, predictive analytics, and trend analysis enable project managers to monitor project progress, identify patterns, and proactively address potential issues.

Benefits Realization Management:

Benefits Realization Management focuses on ensuring that project deliverables effectively contribute to the intended benefits and strategic objectives.

Techniques such as benefits mapping, benefits tracking, and benefits realization plans are employed to align project outcomes with desired business outcomes and measure the actual value delivered by the project.

These advanced project management techniques require a deeper understanding of project management principles, specialized knowledge, and experience. They are typically applied in complex, high-risk, or strategic projects where traditional project management approaches may not be sufficient. By leveraging these techniques, project managers can enhance project performance, mitigate risks, optimize resource utilization, and maximize the value delivered by projects.

10.1 Earned Value Management

Earned Value Management (EVM) is a project management technique that integrates the measurement of scope, schedule, and cost performance to provide an objective assessment of a project's progress. It helps project managers gain insights into project performance, identify variances, and make informed decisions to keep the project on track. Here's an overview of Earned Value Management:

Key EVM Concepts:

Planned Value (PV): Also known as the budgeted cost of work scheduled (BCWS), PV represents the authorized budget allocated for the work scheduled to be completed at a specific point in time.

Earned Value (EV): EV, also called the budgeted cost of work performed (BCWP), represents the estimated value of the work actually completed at a given point in time.

Actual Cost (AC): Also known as the actual cost of work performed (ACWP), Actual Cost (AC) is a term used to describe the costs actually incurred for work that has been completed up to a certain point in time.

EVM Metrics:

Cost Variance (CV): CV indicates the difference between the earned value (EV) and the actual cost (AC), providing insights into whether the project is under or over budget.

Schedule Variance (SV): SV represents the difference between the earned value (EV) and the planned value (PV), indicating whether the project is ahead or behind schedule.

Cost Performance Index (CPI): CPI measures the cost efficiency of the project by comparing the earned value (EV) with the actual cost (AC). CPI greater than 1 indicates cost efficiency, while less than 1 indicates cost overrun.

Schedule Performance Index (SPI): SPI assesses the schedule efficiency by comparing the earned value (EV) with the planned value (PV). SPI greater than 1 indicates schedule efficiency, while less than 1 indicates schedule delay.

EVM Formulas:

CV = EV - AC

SV = EV - PV

$$CPI = EV / AC$$

$$SPI = EV / PV$$

Benefits of EVM:

Objective Project Assessment: EVM provides an objective and quantitative assessment of project performance by considering both cost and schedule factors.

Early Warning of Variances: EVM helps identify cost and schedule variances early in the project, allowing project managers to take corrective actions promptly.

Performance Trend Analysis: By monitoring EVM metrics over time, project managers can analyze performance trends, predict future outcomes, and make data-driven decisions.

Communication Tool: EVM metrics serve as effective communication tools to convey project status and progress to stakeholders, enabling transparency and informed decision-making.

EVM Implementation Process:

a. Define the project scope, WBS (Work Breakdown Structure), and associated activities.
b. Assign budgeted values (PV) to each activity based on the project plan.
c. Measure the actual cost (AC) incurred for completed activities.
d. Assess the completed work and calculate the earned value (EV).
e. Calculate EVM metrics such as CV, SV, CPI, and SPI.
f. Analyze the metrics to identify variances and trends.
g. Take corrective actions, such as adjusting resources or revising the project plan, to address any identified variances.
h. Continuously monitor and update EVM metrics throughout the project to ensure ongoing visibility and control.

Earned Value Management provides project managers with a comprehensive and objective view of project performance, allowing them to proactively manage cost and schedule variances. By utilizing EVM, project managers can make data-driven decisions, take timely corrective actions, and improve the likelihood of project success.

10.2 Critical Path Analysis

Critical Path Analysis (CPA), also known as Critical Path Method (CPM), is a project management technique used to determine the longest path of activities in a project schedule, known as the critical path. CPA helps identify the activities that have the most significant impact on the project's duration and enables project managers to optimize scheduling and resource allocation. Here's an overview of Critical Path Analysis:

Activity Identification and Sequencing:

Identify all the activities required to complete the project and define their dependencies.

Sequence the activities in a logical order, ensuring that each activity has a clear predecessor and successor.

Determining Activity Durations:

Calculate how long it will take to finish each project task. This can be done using historical data, expert judgment, or other estimation techniques.

Activity durations should consider factors such as resource availability, complexity, dependencies, and any constraints.

Constructing the Network Diagram:

Create a network diagram, also known as a precedence diagram or project schedule network diagram, using the identified activities and their dependencies.

The network diagram visually represents the sequence of activities and their relationships, typically using nodes (representing activities) and arrows (representing dependencies).

Determining Early Start (ES) and Early Finish (EF):

Calculate the early start (ES) and early finish (EF) for each activity in the network diagram.

ES represents the earliest point in time when an activity can start, considering its dependencies and the project's start date.

EF represents the earliest point in time when an activity can be completed, considering its duration and the ES of its preceding activities.

How to calculate late starts (LS) and finishes (LF):

Calculate the late start (LS) and late finish (LF) for each activity in the network diagram.

LS represents the latest point in time when an activity can start without delaying the project's overall duration.

LF represents the latest point in time when an activity must be completed without delaying the project's overall duration.

Calculating Total Float (TF):

Total float, also known as slack, indicates the amount of time an activity can be delayed without delaying the project's overall completion date.

Total float is calculated by finding the difference between the late start (LS) and early start (ES), or late finish (LF) and early finish (EF) of an activity.

Activities with zero total float are critical and reside on the critical path.

Identifying the Critical Path:

The critical path consists of a sequence of activities with zero total float (TF).

The critical path represents the longest duration path through the project network, indicating the minimum project duration.

Any delay in activities on the critical path will result in a delay in the project's overall completion.

Managing the Critical Path:

Project managers need to closely monitor and manage activities on the critical path to ensure that they are executed as planned.

Delays or changes in activities on the critical path may require adjustments in the project schedule, resource allocation, or project scope to maintain the project's overall timeline.

Schedule Optimization:

Critical Path Analysis provides insights into the project's schedule dependencies and opportunities for schedule optimization.

Project managers can focus on activities with float or non-critical paths to optimize the project's duration, resource utilization, or costs.

Updates and Monitoring:

Critical Path Analysis is an ongoing process that requires regular updates as the project progresses.

Monitor changes in activity durations, dependencies, and constraints to ensure the critical path remains accurate.

Assess the impact of any schedule changes or delays on the critical path and take appropriate actions to manage the project's overall timeline.

Critical Path Analysis helps project managers identify the critical activities that directly impact the project's duration. By focusing on the critical path, project managers can allocate resources effectively, prioritize tasks, and manage project schedules more efficiently. It enables them to identify potential bottlenecks and take proactive measures to ensure the project is completed on time. Critical Path Analysis is a valuable tool for project planning, scheduling, and control, contributing to the successful execution of complex projects.

10.3 Project Portfolio Management

Project Portfolio Management (PPM) is a strategic approach that involves the centralized management of a collection of projects, programs, and other related initiatives to achieve organizational objectives. PPM provides a structured framework for selecting, prioritizing, and managing projects based on their alignment with business goals, resource availability, and risk factors. Here's an overview of Project Portfolio Management:

Aligning Projects with Business Strategy:

PPM focuses on aligning projects and initiatives with the organization's strategic objectives and long-term vision.

Project portfolios are evaluated based on their contribution to business goals, market demands, financial impact, and competitive advantage.

Project Selection and Prioritization:

PPM helps in selecting the most appropriate projects to be included in the portfolio.

Projects are assessed based on their potential benefits, risks, resource requirements, and alignment with the organization's strategic priorities.

Prioritization techniques, such as scoring models, cost-benefit analysis, or strategic value assessments, are used to rank projects and determine their relative importance.

Resource Management and Optimization:

PPM ensures efficient utilization of resources by considering the overall capacity and availability of resources across the project portfolio.

It helps balance resource allocation among projects, preventing resource bottlenecks and optimizing resource utilization to maximize portfolio value.

Resource management techniques, such as resource leveling, capacity planning, and demand forecasting, are applied to achieve optimal resource allocation.

Risk Assessment and Mitigation:

PPM incorporates risk assessment and mitigation strategies at the portfolio level.

Risks are evaluated across projects, considering their potential impact on the portfolio's success.

Risk management techniques, such as risk analysis, contingency planning, and risk response strategies, are applied to minimize the overall portfolio risk exposure.

Performance Monitoring and Reporting:

PPM establishes mechanisms to monitor and evaluate the performance of projects and the overall portfolio.

Key performance indicators (KPIs) are defined to measure project and portfolio performance.

Regular reporting and review processes provide stakeholders with visibility into project progress, resource utilization, financial status, and overall portfolio health.

Portfolio Balancing and Optimization:

PPM involves balancing the project portfolio to ensure the right mix of projects that collectively deliver the desired strategic outcomes.

The portfolio is continuously reviewed and adjusted based on changing priorities, resource constraints, market conditions, and business needs.

Optimization techniques, such as portfolio scenario analysis, what-if analysis, and sensitivity analysis, are used to explore different portfolio configurations and make informed decisions.

Governance and Decision-Making:

PPM establishes governance structures and decision-making processes to guide project selection, prioritization, and execution.

Governance frameworks ensure that project and portfolio decisions align with organizational policies, standards, and compliance requirements.

Decision-making authority, roles, and responsibilities are clearly defined to facilitate efficient and effective portfolio management.

Benefits Realization:

PPM focuses on benefits realization by tracking the actual value delivered by projects and assessing their impact on the organization.

Benefits management frameworks and methodologies are used to identify, measure, and monitor the benefits expected from each project within the portfolio.

By actively managing benefits realization, PPM ensures that projects align with the organization's strategic objectives and generate tangible value.

Continuous Improvement:

PPM promotes a culture of continuous improvement by regularly evaluating portfolio performance, lessons learned, and best practices.

Feedback and insights gained from project and portfolio performance reviews are used to enhance decision-making processes, optimize resource allocation, and refine portfolio management strategies.

Portfolio Governance Tools and Software:

PPM is supported by portfolio management tools and software that provide centralized visibility, reporting, and analysis capabilities.

These tools facilitate portfolio selection, prioritization, resource management, risk assessment, and performance tracking.

Project Portfolio Management allows organizations to optimize resource allocation, maximize the value of their project investments, and strategically align projects with business objectives. By implementing PPM practices, organizations can make informed decisions, mitigate risks, and effectively manage their project portfolios to drive business success.

CONCLUSION

Mastering the art of project management is a continuous journey of learning, experience, and growth. It goes beyond the technical aspects of planning, scheduling, and controlling projects. It requires a combination of leadership, communication, adaptability, and a deep understanding of both the project and the people involved. As project managers, we strive to deliver successful outcomes while managing constraints, navigating uncertainties, and inspiring our teams to achieve greatness.

To truly master the art of project management, we must embrace a mindset of continuous improvement. We learn from each project, capturing the lessons and insights that shape our future endeavors. We seek out new knowledge, staying abreast of emerging methodologies, technologies, and best practices. We leverage the wisdom of those who came before us, drawing inspiration from successful projects and the experiences of seasoned project managers.

Effective project management is not just about following a set of processes; it is about harnessing the power of collaboration and building strong relationships. We recognize the value of our stakeholders and engage them as partners on the journey. We communicate transparently, listen actively, and address conflicts with empathy and diplomacy. We create an environment where ideas flourish, innovation thrives, and teams feel empowered to deliver their best work.

Mastering the art of project management is also about striking a delicate balance between structure and flexibility. We understand the importance of solid planning, risk management, and controlling project scope. Yet, we remain open to change, adapting our approaches to suit evolving circumstances and customer needs. We know that agility and responsiveness are key to thriving in today's dynamic and fast-paced business landscape.

Above all, mastering the art of project management requires a passion for excellence. It is the unwavering commitment to delivering value, exceeding expectations, and making a positive impact. It is the drive to inspire and motivate others, fostering a culture of collaboration, creativity, and continuous growth. It is the relentless pursuit of success, knowing that every project is an opportunity to leave a lasting legacy.

Finally, mastering the art of project management is a transformative journey that demands both technical expertise and soft skills. It is a constant pursuit of knowledge, a commitment to continuous improvement, and a passion for delivering exceptional results. By embracing this art, we elevate the practice of project management and create a lasting impact on the projects we lead, the teams we inspire, and the organizations we serve.

APPENDIX 1.0

PROJECT MANAGEMENT TEMPLATES AND TOOLS

Project management templates and tools are resources that assist project managers in planning, executing, and monitoring projects effectively. These tools provide frameworks, standardized formats, and pre-designed documents to streamline project management processes. Here are some commonly used project management templates and tools:

Project Charter Template:

A project charter outlines the project's purpose, objectives, stakeholders, and high-level scope.

It serves as a formal document that authorizes the project and provides a clear direction for the project team.

Work Breakdown Structure (WBS) Template:

A WBS breaks down the project scope into manageable work packages and deliverables.

It organizes project tasks hierarchically, facilitating project planning, resource allocation, and tracking.

Gantt Chart:

A Gantt chart is a visual representation of project tasks, timelines, and dependencies.

It helps in scheduling, resource allocation, and tracking progress over time.

Project Schedule Template:

A project schedule template provides a framework for creating and managing project timelines.

It includes start and end dates, task dependencies, milestones, and allocated resources.

Risk Register Template:

A risk register captures and tracks identified risks throughout the project.

It includes information about the potential risks, their impact, probability, and mitigation plans.

Communication Plan Template:

A communication plan outlines the project's communication strategy, stakeholders, and communication channels.

It ensures effective communication among team members, stakeholders, and project sponsors.

Stakeholder Analysis Template:

A stakeholder analysis template helps identify project stakeholders, their interests, influence, and engagement strategies.

It ensures that stakeholder needs and expectations are considered throughout the project lifecycle.

Change Request Template:

A change request template provides a standardized format for documenting and managing project changes.

It captures details about the proposed change, its impact, and approval process.

Lessons Learned Template:

A lessons learned template captures insights, best practices, and challenges encountered during the project.

It helps in documenting and sharing knowledge for future projects.

Project Management Software:

Project management software tools provide comprehensive features for planning, scheduling, resource management, collaboration, and reporting.

Microsoft Project, Jira, Trello, Asana, and Basecamp are a few examples.

These templates and tools provide a structured and consistent approach to project management. They save time, enhance efficiency, and promote best practices. However, it's important to customize these resources to fit the specific needs of each project and organization. Project managers can leverage these templates and tools to streamline processes, improve communication, and increase the likelihood of project success.

APPENDIX 2.0

GLOSSARY OF PROJECT MANAGEMENT TERMINOLOGY

Project: A temporary endeavor with a defined start and end, undertaken to create a unique product, service, or result.

Project Management: Applying knowledge, skills, tools, and procedures to a project in order to meet its needs and reach its goals is known as project management.

Stakeholder: An individual, group, or organization that is affected by or can affect a project's outcomes, activities, or decisions.

Scope: The sum of all activities, deliverables, and requirements that define the boundaries of a project.

Deliverable: A tangible or intangible product, result, or service that is produced and delivered as part of a project.

Work Breakdown Structure (WBS): A hierarchical breakdown of project tasks, deliverables, and activities, providing a structured representation of the project scope.

Milestone: A significant event or point in time within a project that marks the completion of a major deliverable, phase, or achievement.

Critical Path: The sequence of activities that determines the shortest duration for completing a project, considering dependencies and constraints.

Risk: An unforeseen circumstance or event that, if it materializes, could favorably or unfavorably affect the project's goals

Stakeholder Analysis: The process of identifying, analyzing, and managing the interests, expectations, and influence of project stakeholders.

Change Management: The systematic approach to managing changes in a project, including assessing impacts, obtaining approvals, and implementing change.

Communication Plan: A documented strategy that outlines the communication objectives, channels, frequency, and stakeholders involved in a project.

Resource Allocation: The process of assigning and managing resources (e.g., people, equipment, materials) to project activities to optimize project performance.

Quality Assurance (QA): The planned and systematic activities implemented to ensure that project deliverables meet specified quality standards.

Risk Mitigation: The process of developing and implementing strategies and actions to reduce the likelihood or impact of identified project risks.

Lessons Learned: Insights and knowledge gained from past projects that can be used to improve future project planning and execution.

Baseline: A reference point used for comparison and performance measurement, often representing the approved project plan, cost, or schedule.

Project Closure: The formal process of completing and wrapping up a project, including documentation, final deliverables, and stakeholder acceptance.

Project Sponsor: A senior-level individual or entity responsible for providing financial resources, support, and governance for a project.

Project Portfolio Management (PPM): The strategic management of a collection of projects, programs, and other initiatives to achieve organizational goals.

Cost Management: The process of estimating, budgeting, controlling, and managing project costs throughout its lifecycle.

Schedule: A timeline or plan that outlines the sequence and duration of project activities, tasks, and milestones.

Procurement: The process of acquiring goods, services, or works from external sources to meet project requirements.

Stakeholder Engagement: The ongoing process of involving and communicating with stakeholders to understand their needs, address concerns, and build relationships.

Project Governance: The framework, policies, and procedures that provide oversight, decision-making authority, and accountability for project management.

Lessons Learned: Insights and knowledge gained from past projects that can be used to improve future project planning and execution.

Project Manager: The person responsible for leading and managing the project, coordinating resources, and ensuring project objectives are met.

Work Package: A subset of project activities that can be assigned, executed, and tracked as a single unit.

Dependency: The relationship between project activities, where the completion of one activity is dependent on the start or completion of another activity.

Risk Assessment: The process of identifying, analyzing, and evaluating project risks to determine their potential impact and likelihood.

Stakeholder Register: A document that identifies key stakeholders, their roles, interests, and communication requirements throughout the project.

Earned Value Management (EVM): A technique used to measure project performance by comparing the planned value, earned value, and actual cost of work performed.

Issue Management: The process of identifying, documenting, and resolving project issues or problems that may impede progress or impact project success.

Project Initiation: The phase of the project lifecycle where the project is defined, objectives are established, and initial planning takes place.

Quality Management: The process of ensuring that project deliverables meet the specified quality requirements and customer expectations.

Project Integration Management: The coordination and integration of various project management processes, activities, and deliverables.

Lessons Learned Repository: A centralized database or system that stores and organizes lessons learned from past projects for future reference.

Project Constraints: Limitations or restrictions that may impact the project, such as budget, time, resources, or scope.

Project Stakeholder Management: The process of identifying, analyzing, and managing stakeholder expectations, needs, and engagement throughout the project.

Project Risk Register: A document that identifies and tracks project risks, including their likelihood, impact, and mitigation strategies.

Project Closure Report: A document that summarizes the project's outcomes, lessons learned, and recommendations, created at the end of the project.

Project Management Office (PMO): A department or organizational unit responsible for overseeing and supporting project management activities within an organization.

Agile Methodology: An iterative and flexible project management approach that emphasizes collaboration, adaptability, and delivering value incrementally.

Scrum: A popular Agile framework that enables iterative and collaborative project management, particularly in software development.

Kanban: An Agile methodology that visualizes project tasks on a Kanban board, facilitating workflow management and promoting continuous delivery.

Change Control: The process of documenting, reviewing, approving, and implementing changes to the project's baseline, ensuring proper control and minimizing scope creep.

Lessons Learned Workshop: A facilitated session that brings project team members together to share experiences, insights, and lessons learned from the project.

Project Management Software: Tools and applications designed to assist project managers in planning, scheduling, tracking, and managing project activities and resources.

Project Risk Management: The systematic process of identifying, assessing, mitigating, and monitoring project risks to minimize their impact on project objectives.

Project Governance Board: A group of key stakeholders responsible for providing strategic guidance, oversight, and decision-making authority for the project.